The

Encounters to Help You Enter Christ's Inner Sanctum

Micah Turnbo

Table of Contents

Foreword

My first conversation with Micah Turnbo occurred in 2014, sitting at a picnic table under a large oak tree–with acorns occasionally falling and bouncing off the table. I asked him to tell me his story. Micah started at the beginning, when, as a young boy, he had his first encounters with the Lord, angels, and occasionally, other spiritual beings.

In my previous 40 years of ministry, I had learned how to spot a fabricator, so I listened carefully to assess whether Micah had any of the characteristics of a deceptive person. He had none of the signs I had learned to look for. At least, he was fully convinced he was telling me the truth. I asked myself and God if there were any indications that he was deluded. No, Micah was solidly grounded. My final test was simple. I looked straight into his eyes at length while he spoke, and all I saw was Micah looking back at me. I was convinced. He was truthful, he was totally sane, and he was free of any internal work of the enemy. I believed him.

Since that day, Micah and I have grown very close. He is a spiritual son. We met weekly for the next few years. In our first meeting, I told him that I couldn't help him become a better prophet, but I could help him grow into a better man. And he did. Micah has matured tremendously in the past 8 years. That was no surprise. From the start, Micah showed a humble and teachable spirit. People like that grow. Micah attended the simple prophetic class I taught 3 times before I gave it to him to teach. He attended the church for 3 years without complaining before I ever gave him a microphone.

Micah will stretch your thinking, some to the edge of incredulity. If that is you, remember this. Micah is a humble and *teachable man. He has an intimate relationship with the Lord. Unlike some with giftings as powerful as his, Micah is committed to and ministers under the leadership and authority of his local church. He's the kind of man I want to learn from. And because I fully trust him, I am happy to be stretched by his teaching.*

-Van Cochrane, Senior Pastor of Vineyard Northwest Church, Cincinnati, OH

Introduction

You may be wondering about the title. Let me explain.

This inner sanctuary of Jesus is hidden. You cannot find it on your own. Though this place is real, you cannot get there without an invitation. Jesus' blood made a way for you. He is inviting you to the most Holy place—God's sanctum. This sacred inner place is His mind, heart, and ways. It is a place where the indescribable is made known... that is where you are going. God desires to be known and only He can invite you into His inner sanctum.

I'd like to talk to you about intimacy with Jesus and why I focus so much on it. People sometimes think that when I say the word "intimacy", it can mean sexual intimacy or some type of romantic intimacy. That is not what I'm talking about!

I'm talking about heart-to-heart connection. I am talking about face-to-face interaction. I'm talking about when people come together, when friends come together and there is no wall between them. Friends can interpret each other's hearts and express love language without any misunderstanding. Jesus wants to be with us where our hearts are in the same place, our minds are in the same space.

There is also physical intimacy that does not involve any type of sexual interaction. There is a physical intimacy with friends and family that you can experience that is godly, that is pure, such as putting your arm around them or hugging them.

I am descriptive about the intimacy that Jesus and I share. It can sometimes make people feel a little uncomfortable because we have allowed the world to define what intimacy looks like. We live in an over-sexualized culture because that was the enemy's plan.

Heart-to-heart connection, deep friendship—that deep physical friendship connection that you can have goes beyond the world's definition of intimacy. It goes beyond your imagination. It goes beyond what you think could be possible. Jesus said that He calls us friends and friends know each other well!

Jesus wants you to be vulnerable with Him. He wants you to really know Him, not just know about Him. Have you ever known someone so deeply that you know the sound of their steps when they enter a room? Jesus wants that kind of closeness with you because He wants to be known. He wants you to connect to Him heart-to-heart and face-to-face. This is an intimacy that isn't romantic.

Don't be held back by the world's attempts to define intimacy. The intimacy with Jesus that I'm describing is something more substantial; it's something deeper. I want to invite you into what intimacy with God looks like and how you can explore that. It will change your life! It will change the way you look at the world and the way you look at people.

When you're that close to Jesus you will know what His love is like, what His voice is like, and what His actions and emotions are like. Jesus wants to be your best friend. When we describe this friendship, we're not talking about anything sexual or romantic. We're talking about something that's pure and lovely and good.

Jesus is confident in His identity; He appreciates beauty. Jesus is not afraid to express how you make Him feel. He's not afraid to express intimacy, therefore I don't want to be afraid to express that kind of intimacy either.

You may ask what is my purpose in sharing these encounters? The first reason is that I want to bring others into a deeper place of intimacy with Jesus. That's always been my goal. It's not to give these amazing words of knowledge and to speak of mysteries that no one's ever heard. My second reason is that I want to help you to step into God's reality by experiencing Heaven and the beauty of God.

This book will help you enter that lovely intimate relationship with Jesus. As the old hymn, "Turn Your Eyes Upon Jesus", says:

"Turn your eyes upon Jesus,
Look full in His wonderful face,
And the things of earth will grow strangely dim,
In the light of His glory and grace."

Chapter 1

Beginning to Encounter

Chapter Outline:

My Childhood

I grew up with two sisters and a brother. We have always been super close. I have amazing parents who homeschooled us. The reality of Jesus and Holy Spirit was a part of our homeschooling day. However, we were still kids, and sometimes we just wanted to play with our toys, so our mom would encourage us to take Jesus with us when we went to play.

Lately, I've been thinking about my childhood and reflecting on when I was a kid around six years old and seeing in the spirit. I wasn't just super sensitive to the spiritual realm, but I was sensitive to nature itself and how everything that was created had a reason for being. I could feel the emotions of not only people but also the emotions of animals. To me, the reason the clouds moved in the sky was because the breath of God was causing them to move. Watching the clouds move, to me, was a response to God breathing into the world, and the wind blowing around me was spiritual beings such as angels. Even at a young age I could feel the difference between the wind blowing on the earth and the wind of angels.[1]

Growing up was sometimes hard for me because I had very few friends. I was odd and I was different. I got along very well with my siblings and my parents; they believed in the kind of gifts that I carried, and they followed Holy Spirit, however, they didn't fully understand everything that was happening to me.

One time, my mom and dad and I went down to the basement of my grandma's house, and I remember I could see very clearly the people who used to live in the house walking around and having a meeting. I was looking back in time while I was in my current space of time. Sitting in the basement, I could see people talking who were from a time in the past. I could hear their voices and watch what they were doing and see what they were wearing.

I remember I told my mom and my grandma about it. Mom went upstairs and found a black and white photo to show me of the same era that I had seen. So, I was seeing through time, and I didn't even know it.

It was hard for me to really understand what was happening. As a kid of six, seven, or eight years old, I wanted to make friends. I wanted to have friends, but it felt hard for me to make them because I could see what was going on in their families. To me, there was no space and time. When I was with my friends, I would see images of things that they did earlier or what they were playing with in their house. Sometimes I could see their thoughts; sometimes I could see arguments that were going on inside their home. I was overloaded with so much sight, sound, and smell. It was difficult.

I felt lonely but I wasn't unhappy because I have a good family system. I have two wonderful sisters and a younger brother, and they never made me feel like I was a superhero or some kind of odd person. They always welcomed my gifts and the way they operated but it was still kind of hard for me to focus.

Mom always would tell me, "You're smart. You're smart." But sometimes I would get distracted even while learning normal things. All of us kids were home-schooled. The Lord told my mom to homeschool all of us and so she really got to see how each of us was gifted and what the calling was on our lives. I remember she told me that I was a visual learner; that I needed to see things in front of me or draw things. I wasn't very good at auditory learning, but I could grasp things if I could see them. Mom had a whiteboard, and she would write math problems on the board, or if we were doing spelling, she would write spelling words. I remember that the colors stood out to me. She would write in different colors and at some point, she started to understand that colors also helped me remember things. She would write corrections to spelling or grammar in red and use a blue ink pen when she did math or a blue marker when she did math on the board. Those things helped me because I was such a visual learner. I remember her telling me, "Micah, you're very smart. You just need to see it. You just need to see it and then it gets lodged in your brain."

There was nothing wrong with me, I just had a different way of learning. Even to this day, when I journal, I write things down in different colors because it helps me remember. When I study scripture, I always use bright colors because I remember the wording, or I remember how things stood out to me based on the color. I write scriptures in different bright colors, and for my dreams, I write in dark colors like dark blue or black, or a deep orange. I had to learn how to memorize things with color and by visualizing them.

So as a kid, I had to embrace how I learn and understand things. Things like seeing and hearing in the spiritual world and seeing people's thoughts remained and stayed strong and didn't make me delusional or upset or depressed. I really enjoyed it. It was fun being able to listen to the trees talk and watch them sway in the wind. I could feel the trees; I could feel their reaction to the wind.

One of my favorite things was the water. I learned at an early age that water contains memory. I would go to a stream or creek or lake and put my hand into the water and I could see what happened in that lake or that river or who walked around there during a past time. It was cool. I really loved my gifts, but I felt alone in a world of people who didn't understand me.

There were angels and different spiritual beings who were around me. I could talk to some of them, and I couldn't talk to others or some of them wouldn't talk back to me. I remember one time I was sitting in a field and listening to the grass react to the wind blowing through it. I could feel the emotion of the grass, and as I was still and peaceful, I heard the grass say, "Listen. Listen to us. We have things to say."

I went home and said, "Mommy, the grass wants me to listen to it." She would say, "Micah, go back outside and hear what the grass has to say." To me everything was alive. It wasn't just the spirit world, but the earth itself was alive. The grass was more than just grass, the rocks were more than just rocks. The wind and the clouds and the sunlight were living things.

Every child is different. I wanted to tell you a little about my childhood because I believe there are people reading this book who are similar. I'm still like this. I still can hear the trees, the waters, the winds…. I just want to encourage you. Not everybody in this world is going to totally understand you. They're not going to totally get you, and you know what? You're not on this planet for everybody to understand you. That's not why you have a gift. I had to learn that truth. It's not my job to make everyone understand me and what I'm saying or who I am.

But I do want to enjoy life. I do want to enjoy who I am. I do want to enjoy the kind of person God made me to be.

I encourage you to enjoy yourself. Enjoy the way God made you and don't live your life trying to make people understand you. When people misunderstand you and call you weird or abnormal, forgive them quickly. It's not a problem with you, it's just that they don't understand. Maybe one day they will and maybe they won't, but you're not there to live your life for them. You exist for the pleasure of the Lord. You exist because Jesus loves you and He enjoys you and He wants you to be who you are. So, continue to be who you are my friends. I think you're amazing.

Seeing in the Spirit as a Child

At age three or four I started seeing angels. My church would do these performances for New Year's Eve or hold conferences that included dancing. My sisters and mom were on the dance team. During the performance, I would be sitting on someone's lap, watching my sisters on stage and I'd see colors fly over their heads. When they moved their hands, lights would go around their hands. At the time I thought it was lights from the ceiling, but as I got older, I realized the lights were angels. I could also see angels standing against the wall in the back of the room. I called them "the men in the white suits" until I was about 6 years old. My mom finally realized I was seeing angels because when I would talk about the men in the white suits in the back of the room no one else could see anyone standing there.

Sometimes, as part of the special performance, my church had a prop put on the stage that was a throne designated for the Lord. Whenever the church did this, I would see a man sitting there on the throne with white light around Him. It was Jesus. The God of the universe would sit on the throne and watch the show. I'll never forget His smile; He looked so pleased. I thought, "That's a really cool man, I want to meet Him some time." My parents didn't think anyone was sitting there, but Jesus was sitting there the whole time. Those dance performances were my early experiences of seeing in the spirit even before I really could understand. I thought everybody could see the angels and the man on the throne.

Those experiences were the inspiration for my podcast, *Throne Room Talks*. When I was trying to decide what to call the podcast, the Lord said to me, "Remember when you were little, and you saw me on the throne?"

When I was a child and saw Jesus on the throne during those dance performances, the Lord said the sweetest things to me. He would smile and wave and say, "I love you." It would tickle me. That kind of experience was church for me. Even when my church didn't have a performance with the props and the throne, I would see Him walk around and put His hands on people's backs and just be with them. It was amazing to watch people respond to His presence.

Mom

When I was a kid and I had visions or encounters at night, I would wake my mom up. Sometimes I'd wake her up in the morning or sometimes in the middle of the night. She'd sit up, still half asleep, and her hair would be all over the place and she'd say, "Okay, okay." I would say, "Mommy, I had a dream. Mommy, I saw this." She would get a piece of paper and a red ink pen, and she would write down the vision I had seen or what I felt like I heard God say.

Mom taught me the importance of recording my encounters. Every time I would come to her, she would grab a piece of paper and write it down. She made recording encounters a value. I would notice how ideas and revelation would come to her while writing things down. She would tell me, "Micah, when you write things down, more will come to you. There's always more that Holy Spirit is wanting to teach you."

When I would tell my mom about my supernatural experiences, she would say to me, "Micah, go back to your room and tell Jesus, 'Thank you.'" She told me that I should tell Jesus that I really enjoyed the dream or that I really enjoyed the vision or the encounter.

Mom taught me how to be thankful. I encourage you to always express gratitude for the things God gives you, even if you feel like it's not as epic as other people's revelations. Honestly, you really shouldn't compare the revelations in your encounters, dreams, and visions with what other people experience. You should share your encounters and dreams out of a place of joy, not from trying to be significant or to have purpose.

My mom taught me that having gratitude and thanking the Lord always opened room for more to come. I would go back to my room and would say, "Thank you, Jesus. I want more. I really enjoyed the vision. I enjoyed the encounter." And then I would go back to doing what a normal kid would do, playing or whatever.

If you are a parent, something that you can do with your kids is teach them how to value the way God is speaking to them. My mom didn't want to make it a weird thing that I had visions and dreams or that I saw things that she never saw. She never made me feel weird. She taught me how to really love my gift.

I was incredibly blessed to have parents and a family that received me as a Prophet and as a person. I know not every family is like that and I recognize how difficult it is for those of you who don't have that level of family support.

If you have kids or nieces and nephews, you can train or teach them to enjoy the way God is speaking to them. If there was a cycle when you were growing up where you had a family who thought you were crazy, it doesn't have to be that way in your home now. If you have kids, you don't have to repeat what your parents did with you. Create good memories. Create new traditions.

In my teenage years, I would share my visions and dreams with my mom, and then she would ask me questions. It was cool because the Lord would confirm to her a lot of things. The Lord would tell her things that I was going to say before I came to her to share the vision or encounter. She would see or hear ahead of time, and I would give confirmation to it later when I told her.

Mom did tell me that she would often say a prayer: "Please, please guide my son. Please, I don't want him to end up being crazy. I don't want him to end up being crazy." When she would pray that, the Lord would comfort her because in all reality, although my mom and my whole family were prophetic in different ways, they didn't always have a grid for the supernatural things that I was talking about. They needed confirmation and God was good to give them that confirmation.

You can teach your children even if you don't fully have the answers for their gifts! If you think, "I don't know how. I don't know how to really communicate to my son or daughter," remember that they are your child, and the Lord has given you everything you need to raise them.[2] Don't let the enemy come to your mind and tell you that you don't know how, or you've got a crazy son or daughter, or you don't know what they're talking about. The Lord will help you.

Another incredible thing about my mom was the way she asked me questions. She always had a heart to learn; she always had time to learn. She's my mother and she walks in wisdom, but there were things that she didn't know. However, she was willing to learn. Mom had her own journal, and I would see her write in it about some of the things that I said or things that she had learned from me. Isn't that cool?

Mom's attitude taught me that I should always have a teachable spirit. I need to be willing to learn. No one knows everything and they never will. Only God knows everything.

Now that I'm preaching and teaching and doing all kinds of cool stuff, I see my mom in the audience just grinning and learning and taking notes. My mom leads a prophetic intercessors group at my church and yet she always tells me, "I'm under your leadership. I'm following you."

I would not be where I am today if Mom had not taught me the things that she knew. These are the things that turned my prophetic gift into an incredible blessing to the body of Christ. So, moms, if you have supernatural kids—a prophetic kid, a Seer, a kid who is always in the clouds, who has dreams and visions—just know that you are very valuable, and your child needs you. Your child needs your insight. They need your listening ear because just by listening to them and being part of their world, they will turn into incredible, powerful people.

Dad

When I was young, my dad would lie down in the hallway in his bathrobe and pray. He would do this every day around four in the morning before he went to work. Whenever I would wake up to go to the bathroom, I would jump on his back to play, but I also learned to set aside time to spend with the Lord and to pray in tongues from watching my dad. He taught me how to pursue God and how valuable that is.

My dad would say, "Micah, always remember to practice intimacy with God." He had an understanding that intimacy with God was very important, and he set aside time for his prayer life. I learned that from him and so I did what he did. Dad got on the floor to pray, so I got on the floor to pray.

My dad has always given 100% to his family! He showed me what masculinity looks like and he, still to this day, gives me wisdom! I love my dad! He has always been a man of prayer, integrity, and fun!

When I was around 12, I loved listening to my dad's jazz music and watching the angels outside our van window. Dad would take us for a burger or ice cream, and we'd listen to jazz music and drive around, usually after a long bike ride at a park. While the music played, I watched the angels fly by our van, dancing to the music, waving, laughing, knocking on the windows, or just flying next to the window with a pleased look.

Dad would ask, "What are you thinking about, Micah?" I would tell him I was watching the angels fly alongside our car and describe to him what they were doing. Dad would say, "Oh, that's wonderful."

My siblings in the car would say nothing; it was customary for them to hear me talk this way. Amber and Derri were talking about girl things. Lucas was usually listening and would crack some jokes. Just normal life.

The song would end, and I would ask Dad to play it again. The angels like jazz!

Sisters

I would like to introduce you to my sisters. Amber Christina (Turnbo) Kaufman is the eldest of us all. She is also known as the protector, and the second mother, and she brings the family together. She is always ready to give her best, even when she is physically tired. She has a gentle spirit but a fierce sense of justice regarding what is right and what is wrong. She is also naturally skilled at empathizing with others' feelings. Amber and I are a lot alike in how we process things; each of us can be a guard dog when it comes to feeling the depth of the other's emotions.

Amber taught me that there's never a wrong time to listen and that listening requires your whole body. Empathy is one of the most precious gifts when learning to interact with people. There is always something to learn if you take the time to listen; engage and see what you find. Amber taught me that people are worth the extra second, the extra minute to hear and discover. Never assume that you know everything about someone.

I think prophetic people could learn that engaging with people and becoming good listeners and empathizers would only enhance their ability to demonstrate Jesus to the world.

Joy is contagious and delightfully invasive. It comes in, smashing boredom, sadness, and complacency with a hammer. My older sister Derri is that hammer! She is always willing to try new things and have an adventure. Derri can smell fun and taste excitement. Along with the energy she brings into a room, she also carries peace—a wave of inner peace and the ability to raise strength inside a person.

Because she has inner peace, she can be honest when needed and confident when a challenge is present. However, sometimes Derri will need a hug just like everyone else because being full of joy and strength doesn't make you invincible. There were seasons of challenge that I walked through with Derri where she learned to forgive quickly and come back to her inner peace and contagious joy, which is Jesus. Her center is Jesus.

Derri is also a worship leader, but I will not comment on her leading in front of people, which is lovely; instead, I will speak of her ability to lead people from "the secret place". She leads others from the stillness of being in God's presence.

I have learned from Derri that being a leader begins in secret, before God alone. Jesus brings that smile to her face; He holds her completely stable. I learned from her that protecting the core of who you are is valuable. I watched her find that center when things were tough, and she sang to her King who held her.

Playing Transformers with Lucas

My younger brother is Lucas Franklin Turnbo, and we shared a room while growing up.

Sometimes we would turn off the lights in our room to see if we could see the angels. We would have our toys spread out on the floor and wait to see flashes of light, beautiful white lights that would swell and get bigger. When we turned the lights back on, we would find feathers on the floor. My brother used to collect the little feathers left behind by the angels and put them in a plastic bag to save them. In the home in which I was raised, those supernatural activities were welcome.

I often say that Lucas and I were prone to the supernatural world together. The supernatural started with us playing with our Transformer toys or our stuffed animals that we called "the Bunnies".

"Micah, let's play an episode," Lucas would say when he wanted to play. Often our episodes would take hours of playtime. In every episode, however, we always included God, Jesus, and Holy Spirit.

One time Father's presence physically manifested in our room. We sensed Him come in with heat. Our skin was warm, and we felt someone come into the room as we played with our toys. Both of us ran out of the room to tell Mom.

"Mommy, God is in our room! Can you come upstairs?"

Mom politely shooed us away, "No, honey, go back upstairs and play with Him. He is safe; God wants to play with you."

Lucas and I went back upstairs and peeked into our room. God felt so real to us that we expected to see Him standing there. Encountering God during play was such a part of our growing up. Those moments with my brother cultivated my understanding of Father's desire to know us and be part of our lives. Lucas helped open that world for me!

Meeting Jesus

The following encounter is what really started my message on intimacy with Jesus. He wanted me to be His friend before He called me to bring other friends for Him.

I was 11 years old, struggling with my sexual identity. I didn't know who I was or even fully understand what I was feeling, but I knew that having feelings toward other men was wrong.

I was on my bed praying, asking Jesus to help me with those feelings, and I also wanted a friend. I didn't have any friends and the boys my age always called me "fag" or "girl" and never wanted to play with me. I was lying down, asking Jesus to be my friend. I told Him that I would play like a boy plays and not disappoint Him. I told Him that I would not annoy Him either; I just wanted a best friend who liked me.

After praying that, a light illuminated my room, the brightest light I have ever seen! It was so beautiful and warm.

I looked up and saw angels watching me and covering me with their wings. Each feather was soft to the touch. The angels said nothing to me, but they smiled peacefully. Coming down the hallway, I heard someone walking, and I knew it was Jesus. My heart was pounding with a love I had never experienced before.

Then Jesus walked into my room and intentionally gazed right into my heart. His big brown eyes twinkled with so much joy. His hair reached to His shoulders, and His beard sparkled with the gold of heaven. To my surprise, though, He looked very ordinary. He wasn't glowing with light. He looked like an ordinary man who had come in from playing outside. His robe was dirty, His feet had dust on them, and His hands had dirt under the fingernails. He was normal but everything about Him communicated His desire to connect with me. He knelt on one knee to face me and said, "Micah, I would love to be your best friend. If it's alright with you, may I carry you?"

A big smile erupted all over my face when He asked to carry me.

He knew that was a "yes", so He picked me up and carried me for a long time. When He held me, it felt like He was the big brother I had never had. I was safe. Nothing could harm me.

He laid on my bed with me resting on His chest, listening to His heartbeat, and feeling the rise and fall of His breathing. It reminded me of the time in the Bible when John laid his head on Jesus' bosom.[3] Jesus' grip on me was firm and

His body was strong. I felt so safe, so wanted, so protected. I didn't feel alone anymore.

After some time, Jesus said, "Anytime you want to be with me like this Micah, I will come. I will meet with you and hold you. Also, I would like to show you around Heaven and my place of rest too. Would you like that?"

I was too relaxed to speak but my heart said, "yes", and Jesus knew that.

He said, "I will never leave you, Micah. I am always right here."

I spent years battling homosexuality, but that battle is what brought me to a sustained passionate friendship with Jesus. He never did leave me.

Meeting Father & Holy Spirit

One day Jesus walked into the room, grabbed my hand, and said, "Today we are going to meet Father." I was delighted but I didn't quite know what that meant. He held my hand, and we faced the wall opposite my bed. The wall divided as though it had turned into a curtain that opened. There was a massive throne with amazing amounts of emerald light and thunder and lightning and smoke. Father God was just massive; He was huge. The brightest green rainbow was coming from Him and He kept saying His name.

He would say, "I am the LORD who heals! I am the LORD!" and every time He would say who He was, He would explode with power, just a massive explosion of power that would push all the angels back, and then they would tumble forward again. As soon as He would declare who He was, there was another explosion. The word "holy" was coming from the angels around the throne with different variations of the word "holy" and spoken in different tones–none of them were the same.

Everything was alive! I remember seeing that the hairs on my arm and the hairs on my head were alive and seemed to move separately from each other, which was very interesting. The toys in my room were bouncing! He made everything alive!

When He got to the last phrase, "I am the LORD your Father," I wanted to immediately approach Him and be held by Him like a little child in his father's arms. Suddenly my thoughts changed from witnessing this awesome and amazing power to thoughts about how I just wanted Him to hold me. I wanted to run to Him and be held. As soon as He finished holding me with the comfort of a loving father, the wall closed, and everything was quiet. Jesus said, "That is your Father. Tonight, we will meet Holy Spirit."

I met Holy Spirit that same night. Jesus didn't come and let me know when it was happening. Instead, I woke up in the middle of the night and saw a small flame about the size of a softball come into the room, and spin in a circle repeatedly. Then it grew into this massive funnel cloud. I don't know how it could fit in my room, but it was a massive funnel cloud of fire that made the room very hot. The fire was red and gold swirling together like a giant heated tornado and I was inside of it! I could see a brightness inside the tornado; it was light and fire and then a brighter light inside.

A hand came out of the light for me to grab and so I did, and He said, "Hello, I'm Holy Spirit! I'm looking for friends. Will you be my friend?" I said, "Yes."

Then He shrank into that softball-sized fireball and went into my chest.

Nothing seemed different after that experience, which was interesting, but I knew that He had come from inside of me. I realized, "Oh wow, that entire funnel cloud of fire, that massive fire lives inside of me." I wanted to figure that out. How could something so awesome fit inside little me? And then realizing just how much power I had inside of me... well, that was a game-changer!

You're a... HUH? And You Do What Now? (Micah's Answers to Common Questions)

I'd like to answer some common questions about my personal life journey in being a Seer Prophet. My goal in answering these questions is that you would have a better understanding of what my life is like as a Seer and that you would grow in your ability to impact the world in your own prophetic sphere of influence.

Do you see angels all the time?

No, but it sure does feel like it.

When you say that you "see" something, what does that mean?

It means that I physically see it, like I can reach out and touch it. All my five senses are opened when I see angels.

Do you see demons the same way?

Yes, and it is not fun. Yucky little critters. Demons stink!

Can anyone see in the Spirit?

Absolutely, yes! It is something Jesus prayed for us to do. He said that He wants us to behold Him in His glory. (John 17:24)

If I dream or see an angel or demon, does that mean I am a Seer or Prophet?

No, it does not. Everyone has the capacity to prophesy or move in the prophetic, but not all are Prophets or hold an office of a Prophet. The Bible says, "And it shall come to pass in the last days, says God, That I will pour out of my Spirit on all flesh; Your sons and your daughters shall prophesy, Your young men shall see visions, Your old men shall dream dreams" (Acts 2:17, New King James Version). Evidence of the Holy Spirit's power is that all will be prophesying, seeing visions, or having dreams, but it is Christ who calls some into the office of the Prophet (Eph 4:11).[4]

Micah, what steps did you take in beginning your prophetic journey?

Three important keys to beginning a journey to become a Prophet: There is the Calling, there is the Commissioning, and there is the Anointing. It is possible to have the Calling but never receive the Commissioning. A common mistake that people believe is that they are a Prophet because someone else called them a Prophet. No, God will call you Himself personally; people may confirm it, but He is the one who does the Calling, Commissioning, and Anointing.

Calling is when the Lord calls you to be a Prophet, or the Lord identifies you as having the Office of the Prophet. You then enter a training period with the Lord for Him to teach you how to be a Prophet.

Commissioning is when the Lord helps you to understand what message you will carry and sends you out.

Anointing is when the Lord gives you the ability to carry out the commission and do it!

Read the opening chapters of Jeremiah, Isaiah, and Ezekiel. There is an interesting story of when Elijah called Elisha by putting his mantle on him. However,

Elisha was unable to operate in his prophetic office until the Lord put His spirit on Elisha.

So again, are you a Prophet because you see an angel or a vision? No. Are you a Prophet/Seer because someone says you are? No. Instead, I encourage you to pray and take that word to the Lord.

I was confirmed as holding the prophetic office by many other Prophets, but the Anointing did not come upon me until the Lord called me Himself. Then came the Commissioning years later and then the Anointing.

How do you work in conjunction with church leadership?

Favor is important. You must have favor from God AND man. You are only a Prophet to yourself if you do not have favor with the people! Now I know it has been said that you shouldn't seek the favor or the approval of man, and that may be true to a certain point, but there must be a mutual agreement among the leadership team about the prophetic role that you hold. Therefore, favor with man must play a part when working within a church. I will discuss this more in the next question.

Do you belong to a church? Are you received there?

Yes! I am part of a healthy community that receives me and loves me. I stay in community because I need to feel loved and accepted too. I am part of the body of Christ. I LOVE my church! It is so important to be in community. That is where you will receive favor from people. Prophets/Seers need to find a community with which they can have accountability. If you want to grow to full capacity with your prophetic gift, get into a community of believers who will sharpen you and equip you. In my local church, I have trusted friends who know me in my weakness and in my strength. Prophets are not meant to be alone but to have fellowship, so I actively seek out my community for encouragement and accountability.

When you go to Heaven, do you mean "in your mind's eye" or imagination?

No, I leave my body. What that means is that my spirit, which is just as real as my physical body, separates from my body by the Holy Spirit. Paul describes it like this in 2 Corinthians 12:2–4 (NIV), "I know a man in Christ who fourteen years ago was caught up to the third heaven. Whether it was in the body or out of the body I do not know—God knows. And I know that this man—whether in the body or apart from the body I do not know, but God knows—was caught up to paradise...."

When I go to Heaven, I literally leave this earthly realm but go to Heaven in my spiritual body, like John in Revelation 1:10 and 4:2.[5] It is not in my mind's eye, and I am not having a vision, but a real tangible experience. It feels far more real than anything I have experienced. It scared me at first, but I got used to it after a while. Jesus is the one who initiates every spiritual encounter and I only go to Heaven by the Holy Spirit. I cannot make myself go to Heaven, but only make myself available through intimacy with Jesus and living a lifestyle of holiness.

Is it possible to see fallen angels? How do I know I am not being deceived?

This is a great and honest question. Spending time with Jesus is so important. The way I keep my mind sharp is by reading the word of God, and through prayer and fasting.

God is light. Demons or fallen angels cannot produce real light, so if you are spending time in God's light you will recognize a false one when it comes. Do not be afraid; you have authority over them. Shoo them away by the blood of Jesus. Also, the Bible tells us to test the spirits (1 John 4:16). The way I test the spirits is by simply asking if they serve the Lord Jesus Christ. Demons hate that question. It is important to test the spirits because the spiritual world is dangerous without the guidance of Holy Spirit. Not all spiritual beings are good. Stay in the Word of God and stay in intimacy with Jesus.

Do you ever see something you wish you hadn't?

Yes, I have a calling on my life; this calling includes sometimes seeing things that are difficult.

However, Jesus is faithful to minister to me when I need it. He has equipped me to do this, and He takes care of me. There are good days and bad days. Some days the gift just feels too heavy, and I want to stay in my room and not come out. Sometimes I must remember that He has called me to this, and I do not get to choose what the Lord shows me. I've already accepted the calling on my life to be a Seer, and that includes seeing things that are hard to see. In seeing those things that are difficult, it means I am bearing witness to the truth/reality of the spiritual world to help equip the body of Christ into His truth. God is not showing me hard things to be mean, but so I would understand the truth and release it to His people so that they may grow up into the fullness of Christ Jesus. So, therefore, the Lord will take me to Hell or have me see demons so the church would know the powers of darkness, but also the power of the Holy Spirit that lives inside each believer to tear down the kingdom of darkness and release the kingdom of God. It is all worth it in the end.

What is a Seer Prophet?

Basically, it is one who sees the word of God. Seer Prophets will behold the glory of the Lord and proclaim it to God's people. You cannot call yourself to be a Seer; it is God who calls you. Seers help equip the body of Christ. All Seers are a type of Prophet, but not all Prophets are Seers! True Seers want to gaze upon the beauty of Jesus and release that revelation to the body. Nothing compares to His majesty. When a Seer

Prophet is equipping the body, it means that people around the Seer Prophet should be experiencing Heaven and be drawn into the beauty of God.

Why do you share your supernatural encounters so much?

Many people ask me: "What's the purpose of sharing encounters and stories? They sound so fantastic." Some people ask, "Can you bring your encounters more down-to-earth? Why can't you be more practical?" Some people mean well when they ask these questions and some people don't, but I want to tell you two of the biggest reasons why I do it.

The first reason is that I want to bring others into a deeper place of intimacy with Jesus. That's always been my goal. It's not to give these amazing words of knowledge and to speak of mysteries that no one's ever heard. My goal is to bring you into a deeper relationship with Jesus. He has always led me into these encounters because He wants you to love Him. He loves you so intensely and He wants you to love Him intensely.

I share these encounters, these moments I have with Jesus so that you can see how deep a relationship with Jesus can go and what it can look like when you just let go and love Him and let Him be Lord of your life and let Him be the kind of King that He desires to be. Jesus cannot be controlled! He's going to be the kind of King He wants to be. He's going to be the kind of "lover" He wants to be toward you. And He wants you to experience the depth of His love. He wants you to experience what love is like with Him when it's unrestrained, when it's wild, when it's beautiful and exciting, when it's over the top, yet when it's full of gentleness and calmness, when the passion of Him is intense like a fire, and yet like soft warm blankets. Jesus wants you to love Him. I share these stories because He's the focus. Intimacy with Him is the focus.

My second reason, which might surprise some of you, is that I want to take you out of this world and help you to step into God's reality. I want you to see things the way God sees them. I want you to see His perspective. It's not about creating a group of Seers. Sure, sharing these encounters does tend to result in launching some people into their calling as a Seer Prophet, but the fantastic life, the fantastic stories, the wonder, and the excitement that these stories bring you is for anyone who is willing to step out of their box.

We often pray for miracles, or we pray for signs and wonders, and yet there's so much doubt in the world. We get so overcome by our impulses to be afraid or worried. We look around us at things that seem to be darker and more intense, but these stories are here, these encounters are here to bring you into God's reality.

Yes, these are real stories. Yes, they really happened to me: they're not made up. I can't make these things up. My goal isn't for you to fight over whether dragons are real, or whether phoenixes are real. I want you to step into the wonder and vastness of God. I want you to step into the "What if?"

God is getting ready to do incredible things on Earth. Things that even Jesus didn't get to do on Earth, He wants to do through you. What if you are that person? What if you are that person who does things on the earth that even Jesus is like, "Whoa, dude! I didn't even get to be part of that kind of miracle. I didn't get to partner with Father on that kind of miracle when I walked the planet."

The thing that is keeping us from walking in that full expression is doubt. I share my encounters on the Behold Wonder website and in this book to help break you free from that doubt. No matter what kind of personality you have, no matter what kind of mind you have, whether you're a left brain or right brain, or middle brain thinker, it doesn't matter. You could be that person that does things on the earth that Jesus didn't get to do. You get to do the greater things![7]

Behold Wonder is removing doubt from the world. It's bringing up a culture of people who believe, who are fantastic, who are wondrous, who are full of the glory of God, who can see the majesty of God, and who don't have a veil between them and God (2 Corinthians 3:18).[8] They're not living a lifestyle of veils, but full of beauty and joy.

Yes, Behold Wonder is here to see those who are full of the love of God, full of love for Jesus. These people are unlimited. They are fantastic. I believe that's you! I believe you are part of that culture.

That's why Behold Wonder is here. That's why I write. That's why I share the stories of my encounters with God. Amazing things are happening and I'm going to be a part of it, and I want you to come along on the journey as well so that you can be part of the cool stuff that God is getting ready to do.

In conclusion, I pray that you would continue to grow in whatever sphere of influence to which God has called you in the prophetic. Some are called to influence their families, some are called to influence churches, cities, ministries, or nations.

If you are beginning your journey as a Seer Prophet, keep on going! Do not give up! Be healthy and prosper in your journey. If you want to grow in the prophetic, go for it! The ability to see in the spirit, to prophesy, and to have visions and dreams is part of Holy Spirit's plan for building the kingdom of God. Draw near to the Lord in intimacy—He alone will satisfy your heart. I love you all!

[1] "He makes His angels winds, and His ministers a flame of fire." (Hebrews 1:7, English Standard Version)

[2] "God has transmitted His very substance into every Scripture, for it is God-breathed. It will empower you by its instruction and correction, giving you the strength to take the right direction and lead you deeper into the path of godliness. Then you will be God's servant, fully mature and perfectly prepared to fulfill any assignment God gives you." (2 Timothy 3:16–17, The Passion Translation)

[3] "There was reclining on Jesus' bosom one of His disciples, whom Jesus loved." John laid his head on Jesus' bosom or breast in John 13:23 (New American Standard Bible 1995)

4 "And He Himself gave some *to be* apostles, some prophets, some evangelists, and some pastors and teachers." (Ephesians 4:11, New King James Version)

5 "I was in the Spirit on the Lord's day, and I heard behind me a loud voice like a trumpet" (Revelation 1:10, ESV), and "At once I was in the Spirit, and behold, a throne stood in heaven, with one seated on the throne." (Revelation 4:2, ESV)

6 "Beloved, do not believe every spirit, but test the spirits to see whether they are from God." (1 John 4:1, ESV)

7 "Truly, truly, I say to you, whoever believes in me will also do the works that I do; and greater works than these will He do, because I am going to the Father." (John 14:12, ESV)

8 "And we all, with unveiled faces, beholding the glory of the Lord, are being transformed into the same image from one degree of glory to another. For this comes from the Lord who is the Spirit." (2 Corinthians 3:18, ESV)

Chapter 2

Understanding My Identity

Chapter Outline:

Out of Homosexuality and into the Truth

There are many common ways that people say they entered homosexuality. For me, even though I knew and loved Jesus and was raised and homeschooled in a loving family who made the Word of God a part of everyday life, I believed a lie.

The lie was "I am not good enough." I tried to pursue "What does it mean to be good?" but kept listening to the lie that grew into "I'm not good enough to be a man and I don't fit into the status quo of masculinity," until I finally accepted it.

I always had a hard time making friends. I would try and try, and it just didn't seem to stick. The enemy sometimes will use the situations that are happening around you to try to boost his point, but I also remember the Lord would say to me, "Micah, I will be your friend."

I used to have dreams where I was riding my bicycle around the block in our neighborhood and Jesus would be with me, riding a bicycle and talking to me. He really wanted to be my friend. What's interesting is that through those times growing up and dealing with homosexuality, the Lord never left me. I still saw Him. I still had encounters in Heaven with Him even when I had thoughts that did not agree with how He designed me.

I want you to hear me on this: I had encounters even amid being homosexual!

I also dealt with pornography. One time the Lord Jesus walked in on me when I was looking at pornography. He walked through the wall and looked right at me. He picked me up, put a ring on my finger, a crown on my head, and dressed me in a new white garment, then He stood back and looked at me and said, "This is you. This is the real you."

What kind of King does something like that? That just blew me away.

It's His kindness that draws us into repentance.¹ There were so many times when I would stumble and fall into sin. My parents would say, "No, you're a man of God. God didn't create you to be a gay man." My parents were a huge force in this, and my siblings were too. They knew what I was going through, but they also kept calling out my true identity. My younger brother and my two older sisters would also tell me, "No, God created you to be a son, a man of God." In my head, I was thinking, *okay, that sounds cool, but I still have all these feelings. I have all these desires.* I would go to Heaven and think, *I can't talk to Jesus right now; I can't be around the Father right now. Don't they know what I was just thinking?*

One of my favorite experiences with God during this time: I was having a really bad day. I was trying to be good in my thoughts, trying to be good in my desires, and it was just not happening. I heard the Lord say to me, "Son, come here." I said, "No, I'm not going," and turned around. When I turned to look behind me, the walls moved and there was this massive throne and God looking directly at me. He stood up off His throne and shouted at me in complete joy and so much love, "Ah, I love you!" He came to me, and He just picked me up and He swung me around and around again and again.

I tell people that when they see gold dust, it's from getting a big kiss from God because gold dust is all in God's beard. I remember Him swinging me around and around and saying, "I love you; I love you; you are so amazing." He held my face, "You're so amazing, Micah." And I wondered, *"How are You this good?"* There was no lightning bolt striking me to death; instead, it was a big ol' bear hug!

Being gay disappeared for me because I had a mind shift on who I was. There had to be a shift in my mind—a change—for me to really believe. Wow! It's not about being gay or straight, it's about being a son of God. That's who I am in Heaven. That's who I am around the throne: a son of God.

I was honest with Jesus—I didn't hide anything. You can't hide anything from Jesus anyway. I'd say, "Jesus, I am not attracted to women right now. You know that I am attracted to men. That's what I feel and you're telling me it's wrong for me to be this way?[2] So does that mean I have to go and like women now?" Jesus would smile at me, and He would say, "No, you are my son in whom I am pleased. You are my son; live from the reality that you're a son of God."

When I finally reached that reality, homosexuality just disappeared from my life. It wasn't like a massive power encounter; it was just gone. I remember that day walking up to my college class when I realized it was gone! It's not there anymore. It's not even an option or a thought. It's not... it's gone. It's just gone, and I don't want to be anything else. I just want to be His son. I am His son.

Yes, my masculinity is part of the identity of being a son, but I am so much more. In the LGBTQ community, there's a "You need to accept everything about me or you don't accept anything at all" mentality, but I refuse to let culture tell me how I should act or be. Even for the color of my skin—how a Black male, a Black male Prophet should act. No. I am a son who is loved. That's where I live. That's where I stand.

Previously, identifying as homosexual was deep in me, woven into the core of my spirit. I believed that was how I was and that I couldn't change. But that was a lie.

It's all about the love of God. The voice of God sets us free. The voice of God is powerful. It was His voice continually speaking into that deep place, saying to me, "No, this is who you are," that released power, that released love.

My parents and my siblings did their part, saying, "This is who you are, this is who you are...." That's awesome, I needed them to keep saying it to me, but they were not the voice of the Lord. I know they were releasing things in the spirit, but I needed the voice of the Lord to touch me. I needed it to go deep into me and to change and shift and bring me into that new reality. When I was ready for that new reality, I said, "Yes, that's what it is," and the homosexual feelings were gone.

If you are wrestling with homosexual thoughts right now, I want to encourage you to always ask, "Jesus, what do you think of me? Who am I to you? How do you feel about me?"

Jesus and I would go through the Song of Solomon and He would say to me, "Micah, read Song of Solomon 1." I still dwell on verse 2, even to this day. I go back to meditate on it. It says, "Let Him kiss me with the kisses of His word." In some translations, it says "kisses of His mouth". Then it says, "For your love is better than wine; better than the pleasures of this world." I would read that, I would say it, and I would pray out of that verse, "Jesus, would you come and kiss me with the kisses of Your word?"

I didn't even fully know what that meant, but I knew that it was an intimate thing. I knew that I could access intimacy or closeness even when my heart & mind were saying I wanted something sexual with another male. I know that I am still accessing intimacy or closeness with Jesus now, desiring to be known, desiring to be loved. I know there's truth there. I know that's real. I pray that I encounter Him in a real way and for His voice to touch me. His voice is the one that sets us free.[3] It is.

I got so hooked on listening to His voice that I wanted to hear it again and again, and again. When I experienced those feelings of being gay, I would stop praying and start saying, "OK, God what do you think about me right now?" I wouldn't even address the feelings, I would just say, "God what do you think about me? Tell me why I'm so awesome. Tell me why I'm amazing." And He would tell me. "Micah, you're amazing because I did this for you. I put this in you. We're going to do this together. You're going to see me again tomorrow." And suddenly I'd be distracted from those homosexual feelings because I was so hooked on the voice of God. It says in His Word that His thoughts about you are more numerous than the grains of sand (Psalm 139:18). That is a ton of thoughts! "OK God, if you have a lot of thoughts about me, I want to hear them all," I would say. "God, tell me Your thoughts about me."

In the season of dealing with homosexuality, I remember getting caught up before the throne of God. The throne is so amazing! It's full of light, and the steps that lead up to it and the rainbow…. It's powerful with flashes of light and glory but He wants to hold you, to be near you. It's amazing how God is! I remember walking up the steps to the throne of God and Father, who has a habit of doing this to me all the time, picked me up and put me on His lap and I watched Him work. My head was against His chest, and I could feel Him breathing. In those moments, I'm just like a little kid sitting on his daddy's lap.

Father is real. He's not a spirit that you can just pass through. You can know what He feels like. The gems in His physique–it's incredible. I was leaning against His chest, and I saw a journal. "Father," I said, "that's a beautiful journal. What is it?" He said, "That's yours. All the promises are in there that you will complete and fulfill. It's already written." I began to open it up and the journal flipped open to all these incredible things. Father said to me, "See if you can find anywhere in there where I said that you are a gay man." I couldn't find it. There's nothing in there about it. All that was in there was my sonship—who I was as a son, who I was as a bride of Christ, who I was as a priest unto God. Man, that wrecked me! That wrecked me. I said, "Oh, this is incredible!"

He wanted me to look at it. Father said, "You see for yourself what's in there."

"That's not in there, Lord."

"Yeah, it's not."

And that was Him displaying the vastness of His love right there. The incredible vastness of His love.

I wasn't alone in the journey of coming out of homosexuality. I would compare myself to other people's stories where they had an amazing encounter with the Lord and boom! The gay feelings left. But for me, it was 11 years of struggle. It started when I was 11 years old and continued until I was 22 or 23.

I would have these encounters and people would say, "Well, if you're seeing God, why are you dealing with this?" I knew that the enemy would try to poke and prod me, but Jesus never left me. I would be walking up to school in the college dorms and my mind would be trying to do the right thing. I'd look down at my own feet walking and I would see the Lord Jesus' feet walking next to me. And I would gasp, "There He is!" I would look over and there was Jesus just smiling. Jesus is the happiest person ever. He was just smiling, and He'd put His arm around me, and we'd walk to class. He'd say, "I'm not leaving you. I'm not leaving you." He was always there. He was there with me the whole time. The whole time.[4]

Recently, I was reading Song of Solomon 2:3 where it says, "Like an apple tree among the trees of the forest, so is my beloved." I love the Song of Solomon; I read it all the time. When I meditate on that verse, I go into Heaven, and I land on the grass. The grass is so soft and sings when the wind blows through it. Each blade of grass makes the sound of violins. It's beautiful. There are beautiful apple trees and there's the Lord with the light coming from Him like spirals from His body. He's so beautiful! "Oh, there's my King right there. There's the King." I'm walking and angels come and ask, "Who do you love? Tell us about this man that you love so much." That's what stirs angels. They want to know. When they see you walking in intimacy and close friendship with God, the angels want to be near you because they love Him, and you emit this fragrance of Heaven that the angels don't emit. (Angels have their own fragrance, but when we move in intimacy with God, we emit a fragrance in the spiritual realm.)

So, the angels continue asking, "Why do you love Him so much? Tell us about Him. What about Him is so amazing?" And I'm walking down the road and focused on Jesus under the apple tree. Jesus is glowing and He's beautiful and I sit in His shade of delight. Jesus says to me, "Son, I want you to give what you have tasted."

I began to learn more about my ministry. He wanted me to teach, or to share, or to prophesy what I have tasted. I have tasted the goodness of the Lord.[5] I have tasted that bread. I have tasted that apple. Those apples are the sweetness of God. Jesus said, "I want you to prophesy what you have tasted but you've got to come here and sit under the shade with me." It was so cool!

Psalm 36:9 says, "Within you, is the fountain of life." He wants us to keep coming back to that fountain. I've seen it. In the gardens of Heaven, He will sit on a three-tiered fountain. He's there—He's so awesome! He's there and I think, "There's Jesus! I'm going. I'm going!" And I go up to Him and I sit by that fountain, and He says, "Would you like something to drink?" And I say, "YES!!! Yes! Yes! Yes!" That's what He wants. He wants us to continually come back.[6]

When the homosexual feelings were gone and I told my family, it was like a "Hey, I went to the store and grabbed some bread" conversation. My mom and my dad believed so much that I would get free. I remember telling my brother, who'd been my roommate in college, "Lucas, the feelings are gone," and he said, "Awesome, what did you expect? Of course, they're gone."

It was such a launching into what I'm meant to do and the realness of God. 11 years of going through the journey of coming out of homosexuality and after that season, I experienced a seven-year dry period, but that's what started the ministry of being a friend to Jesus. I understood what friendship looked like with Him. I understood His loyalty, His kindness, and His grace. I understood what His friendship was like, and that understanding shifted and shaped the prophetic voice that I now carry.

Many of us can identify with the lie of unworthiness. Culture says what a man should look like. I remember Jesus appeared to me in my room and said, "I will show you what masculinity looks like." That shifted me. All those encounters and still I had to walk through that understanding of masculinity. I still had to see the fulfillment of His words. I said, "Whoa! My masculinity is defined by Jesus: who He is as a man." I started to read the gospels and read and read and read how God and Jesus defined themselves as men. I said, "OK, there it is right there. I've always been an intimate person. I've always been that way. I have always loved to be close; I love to express intimacy and I was told that men don't do that. But I'm here reading the gospels and seeing so much love and expression of love in how God is describing His love for the people of Israel." Father says things to His people like, "Come, I'll carry you like the lambs" and "Let Him kiss me with the kisses of His word" and "You're the bride, I'm the groom. Our bed is full of spices." I would read all that kind of stuff and realize that what culture is saying about masculinity isn't computing with what God is saying about masculinity.

My favorite color was pink when I was growing up. Why? I loved the brightness of it. I loved the way it made me feel. Boys my age said, "Oh, you're gay" and "Guys don't like that color." Well, I do like that color. When I get essential oils, I enjoy the roses. I want to smell like roses. I am so firm and so complete and so set in my masculinity because I am looking upon Jesus. When I'm looking upon Jesus, I see myself in Him. I see who He is and that sustains me. That holds me because culture is continuing to throw ideas. The spirit of this world is continually throwing ideas of what love looks like, what masculinity looks like, and what femininity looks like, but I'm saying we need to look at Jesus.

I remember when I was doing an internship at the International House of Prayer in Kansas City at the age of 19, when Jesus said to me, "I want friends. Bring me friends." I said, "Okay, Lord, what do you mean by that?" He said, "I want to be known" and tears came from His eyes. I remember the feeling of the tears hitting my hands and He said, "I want to be known. I want them to know what I'm thinking and to know what I'm feeling." And then He said, "Son, you must be close to hear my heartbeat. I want friends who will lay themselves on my chest and hear my heartbeat."

When He said that it reminded me of when I was 11, at the beginning of the homosexual struggle. I had an encounter with Jesus—the first time I saw Him. He came into my room, picked me up, and held me close. He put me on His chest, and He lay down on my bed. I heard His heartbeat and I just lay there for the rest of the night. When I woke up in the morning He was gone. I went downstairs and told my mom that I saw Jesus.

"What did you do?"

"I laid on His chest and heard His heart."

Then she said, "Go back and tell Jesus thank you."

That's one thing my mom always said: "Go back and tell Jesus thank you." I made a habit of it.

Later, when the Lord told me to bring Him friends, I said to Him, "Oh Lord, okay, but a lot of Prophets do floods and comets and earthquakes. Don't you want to do that?" I asked this because I was still trying to figure out what to do as a Prophet. He just smiled. Jesus is so kind. He just smiled and said, "I have something better. I want you to bring me friends. I said, "Lord, I'll do it. You speak to my heart, and I'll do it."

That's where everything began with Behold Wonder. All of it started from that place of bringing people into intimacy and close friendship with God.

I Am a Son

I have been pondering from where I have come, and through what the Lord has brought me in my past. I want to share something that is important to me, and it is about my identity. God is beautiful; we have a story together! Jesus has been my best friend through every heartbreaking situation. Holy Spirit, the most brilliant consciousness that lives inside me, never left. Instead, He guided my heart into the truth about my identity. As I share with you, I hope you find encouragement and freedom in the following words.

I was 11 years old when I first looked at pornography. I didn't completely understand porn, or that it was even a real thing. I felt pressure fall on my head while something invaded my spirit that had no right to be there. I felt a weakness inside me that I wasn't aware of until later. I sat in front of the computer while image after image went by. It was filling something in me that I didn't know was there.

I remember my fingers were shaking and sweat ran down my face while darkness clouded my heart. Yes, Satan lied to me. He deceived me into questioning my sexuality and identity! I was looking at gay pornography that day because, in the small room in my heart, I heard the lie that I was too weak; I wasn't good enough. That lie said I would never be strong enough—no one would ever like me. Demons told me Jesus would leave forever, and that I was not good enough for Him.

See, I had wonderful spirit-filled parents! No one touched me perversely. I had a healthy relationship with my dad... I had everything, but it all began with a lie.

Now, I cannot go into the full story because that would take too long, but I struggled. I felt alone at times, and I felt confusion more than desire. I battled with homosexuality for 11 years! I fought with the demons that said I was gay or that God created me to be gay. I remember asking the Lord how He felt about me. He spoke to me so peacefully, "Micah, I did not create you to be straight or gay; I created you to be a son of God. You are so much more than what you think you are." His calming words rushed into those secret rooms in my heart. Surprisingly, He told me that when I was 14 years old, but the battle did not instantly stop. I had to hold on to the truth with my dear life because it was going to get wild.

Yes, I still saw Heaven. I was still talking to angels, the saints of God and even standing before the throne during those difficult times. I had a wonderful supporting family to help guide me into truth… not the lie. They never called me "gay" in their hearts. They called me by my name! Powerful! They called me into the truth God spoke over my life. Those long years of walking with Jesus were so personal because He had to be the one to take me through it all.

There was a day when I was engaging in pornography. I felt no sorrow for that at all; I wanted to look at men sexually. At that very moment, the Lord Jesus walked right into my room.

Jesus caught me!

There was no turning back now. What was Jesus going to do to me? I closed my computer waiting for His response. He just looked into my eyes, reading every part of me! Then Jesus picked me up and held me close! His words were this, "My son, I am not angry with you. I only see my righteousness in you. Tell me, what do you need? Let me help you, Micah." His voice began to shake with emotion, "Please let me help you." I began to weep hysterically as His presence went into me. His sweet voice encouraged me, "If you died still engaging with this lie and sin that I so generously took away from you on the cross, I would still love you with all my affection! You will always be my first choice, son."

Jesus stepped back and left.

My world shook: in my mind I heard the demons screaming around me. "Jesus, I do not know you." I cried out; "I do not know you!" What is this intense love that destroyed every wall that I have built?

You would think that after an encounter that powerful, the feelings for homosexuality would have left, but they did not. I still felt the emotions, thought the thoughts, and even looked at pornography again, but I started to understand my identity more because I saw who Jesus is!

Something had changed! I was seeing who I was in Him. His love gave me the strength to say "No" little by little every day! Do you know why? I did not see myself as gay or straight! I was seeing myself in the eyes of Jesus!

Now, this is not an excuse to say that Jesus accepted my struggle with sin. No! I am loved so much that He speaks the truth. I am royal; He loves me, I am valuable, and His love is everlasting. His truth is what gave me the strength to resist the lies of the devil! His truth gave me the power to put aside my flesh and walk with Him.

Thus, Father, Jesus, Holy Spirit, and I began our journey toward wholeness! We walked together, we cried together, and laughed a lot! When I failed, Jesus was right there in the dirt with me. My Father was always ready to hug me whenever I needed it, and Holy Spirit wouldn't let me get away with any lie! He is the master of speaking the truth.

Yes, I walked this road. I know the demons, I know the lies told to you, but I am here to encourage you that I am a free man of God! I am so much better than "straight"; I am a son of God! I am healed, free, and loved powerfully! Jesus has taken away the darkness of my sin and carried it for me! I live in His righteousness! I am here to tell you that homosexuality does not have to be your identity: God has more for you!

Set Free into My Identity

Do you know what's so amazing about the love of God? He sets you free and brings you into your identity.

I used to be a gay man. It's true. God set me free from it. I was always a Seer, even when I dealt with these struggles. Father never left me; Jesus never turned away from me; Holy Spirit always was my companion.

What happened?

Their love brought me into truth. The blood of Jesus is powerful! The kindness of God brought me into repentance. Holy Spirit spoke into my heart about my identity as a man of God, as a Bride of Christ.[7]

God did pass His judgment over my life, He showed justice, and His verdict was "MICAH, YOU ARE FREE!"

Am I gay anymore? No! God destroyed that desire.

Do I desire other men? No, it's not even an option anymore. I am so much more.

Does having an attraction to a woman determine my identity? No, it does not. You are so much more than who you are attracted to.

Jesus' blood has set me free and it's so worth being who I truly am! I refuse to let culture tell me what kind of man I am. I refuse to let the culture of this world tell me how I should act because of my skin color. I refuse to let any voice tell me who I am to be. Only Jesus! Only Him.

So, what am I doing now? I write about His goodness. I prophesy the heart of God to His people. I meditate on His word day and night. I see dimensions beyond human description. I talk with angels, fly on giant eagles, and converse with dragons. I melt demons with the fire of God. I teleport physically to places to prophesy to people. I walk in intimacy with God. I behold the glory of God.

I am so much more than what the god of this world tried to tell me. I am who God designed me to be! I am His son and His bride.

I am going to be me. That's it. I am going to be me.

Tag along with me, my friends, if you want to know more. There is too much Jesus to keep to myself!

God's Glory: My Way Out of Porn

There was a moment when I was looking at porn more than three times a day. I still also saw the supernatural realm regularly, but I knew how to switch off my gift when I looked at porn so I wouldn't see demons.

Pornography attacks the place of encounter, and encounters with God are meant to feel good. God's goodness is fantastic. It's His glory. My friends, you are designed to feel good. Pornography is a lie from demons to pull you out of experiencing the creator of glory and goodness.

When overcoming pornography, it is not about grit or strength. It is not about abstinence; it's about consistent encounters with God's presence. I needed to step into His presence even harder.

Jesus told me after repeated failures, "Micah, you looked at pornography five times today; that means I want to give you ten encounters with my glory. The only way forward is to choose something better. What I have to offer you is extraordinary." A small doubtful "yes" would come into my heart after He said this because I had thought He was ready to smite me and talk about my sin.

The realm of glory would open in front of me; angels would pour through, I would see the throne, and Jesus himself would lead me by the hand toward our heavenly Father. I was amazed; the shame of pornography was gone. The wonder returned and the intensity of His love washed over me. The bliss I felt coming from the glory of God was overwhelming! It felt good. Better than good.

Jesus said to me, "You wonder why I am not talking to you about your sin." He pointed to himself, "My kindness draws you into repentance. Your eyes are meant to behold beauty and glory. Your repentance is looking upon me."

That was my way out of my sin. The glory of God was just better than pornography. To those who struggle with porn, it is not the end. There is a way out! It is through encounters with God's glory.

In Exodus 33:18, Moses asked to see the glory of the Lord, and God revealed His goodness to him. Your desire to feel good is not the problem. His goodness is what you need to rise above the temptation of any addiction. If you struggle with porn twice a day, God has four encounters He wants to give you in His glory. That's how radical His love is. He wants to pour out His goodness even more upon you! He is not advocating that you stay in sin; He wants you to choose something better, which is only found in His presence.

Here is where you must make a choice. It is not about the things to which you say "No"; it's about the things to which you say "Yes." God will offer you His glory as many times as you need or desire, but you have to say "Yes."

I would feel the urge to look at porn most often in the morning, so I knew that was the time to encounter God. Every morning I would wake up with a prayer from Exodus 33:18, "Lord, show me your glory." Even today, my visitation times with Him are in the morning, though the desire for porn is not even a question. All I want is to see His glory. Honestly, I am in visitation with God more than three times a day now. You can live this life too. It just takes consistency.

So, schedule your encounter times with God. Yes, create a schedule with God when you will encounter His glory. This will enhance your prayer life. Be consistent, pay attention to when the impulse to look at pornography is likely to happen, and schedule time with God in those slots!

If you fail, don't run away. Immediately run into God's presence. He wants you with Him no matter what. The hardest part for me to accept was when the glory realm would open to me after I failed. Angels would invite me into Heaven. God wants you with Him no matter what; I had to give in to His invitation and trust His love even after I sinned. Those times were the most powerful moments with God.

You were made to see His glory and experience His goodness all the time. Beholding His glory is the way out. My friends, your impulses do not control you. God has given you the power to overcome this, and your power is the glory of God. Behold Him with all you've got. The way we defeat pornography and every spirit of addiction we have is to look up and behold the glory of God.

Prayer: In Jesus' name, I call to the heavens around you and above you, step into encounters with God's glory. Jesus, you have defeated pornography by the power of your blood. I prophesy over you that it is time to come into His glory. In Jesus' name. Amen!

Satan's Final Words

Satan's final words to me when I left homosexuality behind were surprisingly enlightening.

Jesus stood on my right while Eden, my guardian angel, stood on my left.

Satan looked down on me like a bully would do to dominate and stir fear, "You know why I attacked you? Do you want to know why I tried to take away your identity? Because every time I looked at you, I would see Him. You smell like Him. You remind me of everything good, and I hate everything good. You are so perfect." Satan spat at my feet, "You are so perfect. And I hate you. I have lost everything...."

Jesus watched Satan with a blank cold stare. His eyes never blinked.

Satan continued, "I want to destroy all people, and destroying you was an attack against Him." Satan, pointing at Jesus but never looking Him in the eyes said, "In destroying you, I would have destroyed Him. I know my day is coming when I will leave this world, but I will take many with me. I will take many with me to come against..." Satan stuttered as even the name of Jesus weakened him, "Him... And you." Satan turned to Jesus, "You win. You have your little boy. Your special little king. But I remember all the thoughts he had. I know how dark his soul went. I know the things he wishes not to remember, and I will remind him of it all. He may be standing next to You, but he will always be mine."

Jesus finally blinked. He lowered His head and laughed at Satan. He tilted His head to the side with a smile, "You are so crafty, Satan. I know, I created you. You have always been just words. You wanted to see if I would lose this one, and I didn't. I won. Now you are wasting my time."

Jesus stood behind me and placed His left hand on my shoulder while extending His right hand in front of me in the form of a gun, pointing toward Satan and He quietly spoke the word, "Bang."

A great force pushed Satan into a darkness that appeared as vicious claws grabbing him and pulling him away.

Satan screamed in rage as his eyes became blood-red from his anger toward the Lord and me.

I watched the darkness swallow him, and Jesus placed His right hand on my shoulder and said to me, "You belong to me, Micah."

Again, I believe that there is freedom from this sin. God set me free, and Satan has never touched me with it again. Memories of this sin have no power over me. That's all they are: just memories of where I came from and how my greatest friend Jesus stood with me the whole time. I am not afraid of the memories. On the contrary, I treasure them because they are filled with God's presence helping me overcome that sin by the power of the Holy Spirit.

Jesus won! I belong to Him. I walk in Christ's perfection!

You are Powerful

You can resist the enemy by your choice. You are not weak; you are above, not beneath. In this encounter, Jesus talks about your choice, compromise, and holiness. Hear His thoughts about you and just how powerful you are!

There are moments when Jesus and I sit together on our simple white bench in Heaven. I can smell the roses in the garden and hear the birds singing. Jesus is absolute beauty; the purest of light dances all around Him. His complexion is so radiant that it feels like you are looking right into the sun, yet it's very pleasing to the eyes. Jesus is so pure and there is no shadow in Him. His robe is living light, and a rainbow flows around Him like a river. Jesus, you are beautiful! I was resting my head on His shoulder when He said, "Son there is something on my heart to share with you today. Will you hear it?" I sat up and held His hand to show that He had my full attention. His precious blue eyes looked deep into my heart like He wanted to connect on a level that only God and creation can.

He said, "Son, do not blame the enemy for your decisions. He cannot control you. You make the decision to choose darkness or to choose light. I have redeemed you, and that is also your ability to choose. I have given you authority over Satan." He paused a moment to let His words sink in, "Darkness cannot live with light. Sin cannot live with holiness. I will judge darkness, my son. I will destroy it forever, so it shall not take form or gain hold ever again. There is no sin in my kingdom and no shadow among those who love me. I have set you free from all darkness—your purpose is to please me and stay in my light. Darkness is defeated when you rest in the light of my presence."

His voice carried authority when He spoke the following words: "Compromise is the same as deception; stay away from it. Compromise releases evil spirits!" He placed His hands on my shoulders, "Live in the light as I am in the light. Holiness is not a religious spirit. Holiness describes me and how I have called you. Do not confuse the religious spirit with holiness. The religious spirit comes from fear, but holiness comes from love! When I commanded you to become holy as I am holy, I wanted you to become love and love is light. Love casts out all fear."

I was still thinking about all His words about how the enemy is darkness and how he is evil. He is the one who wants to destroy us. He causes evil in the world.

Jesus replied to my thoughts, "Yes, he is evil, but you still can choose. I made a choice to fulfill my Father's will when Satan came to tempt me. You have the freedom to choose darkness or light. You are powerful, Micah. I live inside you." We stood up to walk the diamond path when Jesus said, "You are stronger than you know, Micah. The enemy can only manipulate you into thinking he has more power than you."

I was pondering about how I blame the devil for my decisions when I have the power of choice. I give him credit, or I accept the lie that he is stronger than me. I had let him tangle me in lies. Jesus smiled, "I am faithful to forgive and bring you into the freedom I have already won for you." He firmly placed His arm around me, "You are a son of God! You are above and not beneath. The enemy hates your ability to choose, never let him make you believe you cannot choose."

Jesus finished speaking, and suddenly, I was back in my room thinking about everything I had witnessed, when Holy Spirit said to me, "The power of God lives inside you. You have the power to climb every mountain, to resist every temptation, to ignore every lie! You are strong and I will remind you of that strength every day."

Breakthrough Keys to Getting Free

One of the greatest breakthroughs I had on my journey to becoming sexually whole was understanding that just because

I deeply love another male doesn't mean I am gay. The definition of intimacy is closeness or close friendship, even though our culture tends to give a sexual connotation to the word "intimacy".

The way God has fashioned me brilliantly is that I can love my guy friends and be close to them without sexual attraction.

Satan is such a liar. He deceived me into thinking that just because I desired to be close to my best friend, it meant that I had same-sex attractions. His lies caused me to worry that because I hugged my best friend for longer than ten seconds, I would get an erection. His lies made me think that I would lose control over my feelings and thoughts. His lies made me think that I wanted to have sex.

He always made it seem that I had a problem, and the only way that I could be "free" was to accept that I was gay.

No! Being gay is not a solution. It's a lie, an alternate lesser version of the real you.

If I want to be sexually whole the way that God created me to be, I need to embrace the emotional side of me as a man. Jesus prayed in John 17:21 NIV, "that all of them may be one, Father, just as you are in me, and I am in you. May they also be in us so that the world may believe that you have sent me." So, Jesus desires that you and I would have the closeness, the emotional and spiritual connection, that the Father, Son, and Holy Spirit already enjoy. Therefore, my desire to be close to my friend was not sexual but rather spiritual! There was nothing wrong with me wanting to hug my friend tightly or to say "I love you" every time I saw him. There was nothing wrong with holding my dear friend's hand when we talked.

There was nothing wrong with my thoughts of wanting to connect or be emotionally close. Jesus wants me to be close to others, not distant. Jesus wants us to be one, not in a sexual sense, but in a spiritual unity that breaks the bondage and the lies of the enemy.

I had to understand that the enemy was jealous of me, and he was jealous of my ability to connect.

Not everyone will see intimacy as I do, and I understand that everyone has boundaries with what's comfortable for them. Just because someone has different physical boundaries than you do for expressing love within a friendship doesn't mean you have a problem. You are just different in a beautiful way.

It took time for me to understand that other men are not in the same place as I am when it comes to expressing friendship and brotherly love. But that's okay with me.

Do not let the enemy deceive you into believing the lie that there is something wrong with you. In my case, the deception was that I was gay and that no man should ever show any kind of physical affection unless he was gay. That lie led me into sexual brokenness.

When I embraced myself in the way God designed me according to His word, I began to heal, and enjoy the level of close friendship or intimacy I can have within my friendships.

Satan has tried so hard to ruin true intimacy with lies. I believe we will see a restoration of what healthy intimacy looks like. I believe healthy relationships are a sign that the Kingdom of God is near.

Victory

One of the best things I learned while walking into my freedom from homosexuality was that I had to pursue my freedom for myself. The journey was between the Lord and me. I wanted to be what God truly made me to be in Christ Jesus.

Listen, you must work hard, fight hard, and stay true to what the Word of God says, not to what anyone else says. Hold onto the love of God, which is holy and gentle.

One of the most difficult battles I faced was dealing with gay pornography. I know this is a tough topic. So many people battle with same-sex porn, and I want to encourage you that you can get free from it. Do not fight the battle alone; ask for help. Cry out to God and He will answer you. Often, God will answer you through trusted friends with whom you can share your struggles. Do not forsake those relationships that challenge you and call you closer to your identity in Christ.

I love martial arts very much; my journey into sexual wholeness reminds me of it. When I studied martial arts, I took away three critical skills that helped me to overcome: focus, strength, and dedication. These three things helped me walk through the challenge. Focus on God. God is my strength. I dedicate my life to His work.

I am praying for you! You have the victory; don't give in. If you fall, get back up and keep trying! The enemy is terrified of those who rise when they fall. You have unlimited strength in God, which leaves the enemy powerless against you. Keep standing up!

I'm a son of God who is walking in his destiny as a Seer Prophet to the nations! I ignite hearts into a brighter flame of love for Jesus. These are eyes who have seen the King of Kings!

I was gay and now I'm not! I was lost in my suffering and now I'm free to be who I truly am in Jesus!

I am a warrior! I am a bride of Christ who is passionately loved by God.

And yes, one day I will marry a beautiful strong woman because God is good!

God set me free! And He will do it for you too!

1 "...do you think lightly of the riches of His kindness and restraint and patience, not knowing that the kindness of God leads you to repentance?" (Romans 2:4, NASB 1995)

2 "Flee from sexual immorality. Every other sin a person commits is outside the body, but the sexually immoral person sins against his own body." (1 Corinthians 6:18, NIV)

3 "Out of my distress I called on the Lord; the Lord answered me and set me free. The Lord is on my side; I will not fear." (Psalm 18:5–6, ESV)

4 "It is the Lord who goes before you. He will be with you; He will not leave you or forsake you." (Deuteronomy 31:8, ESV)

5 "Oh, taste and see that the Lord is good! Blessed is the man who takes refuge in him!" (Psalm 34:8, ESV)

6 "...but if anyone drinks the living water I give them, they will never be thirsty again. For when you drink the water I give you, it

becomes a gushing fountain of the Holy Spirit, flooding you with endless life!" (John 4:14, TPT)

[7] "For your husband is your Maker, whose name is the Lord of hosts; and your Redeemer is the Holy One of Israel, who is called the God of all the earth." (Isaiah 54:5, NASB 1995), and "For the husband is the head of the wife even as Christ is the head of the church, His body, and is Himself its Savior." (Ephesians 5:23, ESV)

Chapter 3

Beholding His Beauty

Chapter Outline:

- The Beauty of Father
- The Beauty of Jesus
- The Beauty of Holy Spirit

The Beauty of Father

I ask that you open your imagination so God can "enlighten the eyes of your heart" (Ephesians 1:18). Ask Holy Spirit to show you our mighty Holy Father. Ask Him to destroy your box of preconceptions of God so you can jump into the fullness of His love. Enjoy!

I was in prayer one afternoon asking Holy Spirit to show me the Father. I wanted to see Him again. I prayed and worshiped God. After some time, I stopped to rest and suddenly I was flying through a portal of golden light. I passed millions of angels moving up and down around me. It was wild, but I was not afraid. I was so excited to see my Father.

As I traveled in the brilliant light, I came up from under the crystal sea and landed before the glorious throne of God.[1] I was alone, with no angel or person in sight. It was just me standing on the calm sea before Father who was looking at me. I could hear Him breathing and was overwhelmed by His presence!

The glory of God is infinite and indescribable. He is an astonishing white light, brighter than a trillion suns. You can see all beauty moving out of Him in waves of different colors, lovely sights, and fragrances. He is all! He is "the" wonder! He fashions every reality from His hand. His hair is perfectly white, and His "skin" is like the gathering of diamonds sparkling by light. His face is full of radiant love which draws you into His eyes of blue fire. I can feel His heart toward me. All I want is to be in His arms forever. He is love and He is happy. There is a rainbow of perfect green light that circles Him—amazing! God is life; He is eternity! You can see eternity and infinity coming from Him and moving in and out of you. Liquid light moves up and down Him like a garment. Sparks of fire dance all over Him and spread out from His presence. Flashes of blue and red lightning come from His hands and feet. He is holy!

I saw His robe flow down the golden steps that lead straight up to the throne of light. Father leaned forward and brought His hands together saying, "Micah, would you like to spend time with me?"

I ran to Him as fast as I could until I was swept up into His arms. He whispered sweetly to me, "Micah, stay here with me." I felt His big warm hands hold my head as a father does to His child. I looked into His eyes of love. He said to me, "I do not see you as you see yourself, my son. I see you as a gift to my heart. I see you as my joy, my love, my wonder to the highest heavens and to the deepest parts of the earth. My light made you; I formed you in the deepest place of my soul." He pressed me against His chest to rest; I could feel Him breathe. God's hands rested on my back, "You are my son. I am your Father. I do not want you to give this truth away for lies of the world. You will forever be my son and loved with an everlasting love that darkness cannot take away. I did not create you as a slave, Micah. I created you to rule with my Son and walk in His inheritance. I created you to stand up in me and walk into eternity. I created you to live forever in life with Me."[2]

Father took a deep breath and said, "Life, my son. I created you for life. Live in joy, live in peace, live in love. Living as a son of God means living in me. Walk in love, walk in peace, walk in joy. My joy causes the enemy great fear. My peace causes the enemy great anxiety. You are free! Living in my freedom puts the enemy in chains!"

I sat up to look at my Father. He smiled while gently touching my face, "If they only believed in me as I believed in them, son. I am not who they think I am. My church has decided to give me an identity instead of letting me show them who I am. I am patient, I am kind, I am slow to anger, I am compassionate, and I am fun![3] I do not turn you away. You are my joy, and I am yours." He paused and looked out toward the sea, "Micah, look!" He turned me around to see a spectacular view of Jesus approaching us.

Oh, my heart was so full of love for Jesus! He is coming! Jesus!

Father whispered into my ear, "Micah, I am so happy for both of you! I long for the day when you dance with Him. He is the desire of all nations. I have given you as an ally of great power and strength to my Son!" Jesus stood waiting at the bottom of the steps watching me with joyful expectation.

Father said, "Do you desire this, Micah?" I laughed in response because I felt so much joy. Father laughed too. I guess my answer tickled Him. He looked toward Jesus with a joyful shout, "It is my pleasure to present to you my son, Micah, the joy of my heart!" Jesus opened His arms to receive me. Father placed His hand on my head to say, "Micah, there is no greater destiny than this. Chase not the dreams of the world. Love my Son, love Him well, and He will fulfill the desires of your heart."

"NOW GO!" Father exclaimed. I stood up and held onto His hand until we released each other while I descended toward Jesus. I could feel Father waiting for my next return to His lap. He said, "Go and come back to Me... you are my joy!"

I walked down the golden steps and stood in front of Jesus. He held my right hand while His glory washed over me. Jesus looked into my eyes with amazement, "My friend, I see my Father's beauty in you!"

The Beauty of Jesus

No other king moves my heart as He does. Sometimes my soul yearns for the touch of Jesus. He is perfect! Part of my calling as a Prophet is to shift and challenge people's understanding of how much God loves us! Jesus' love for us is beyond comprehension; it "surpasses knowledge" (Ephesians 3:19)⁴. I ask that as you read this you open your imagination. Ask Holy Spirit to take you into your imagination to the place where His glory dwells.

The two angels who waited with me were silent because of what was about to happen; they wanted my attention to be only on Him. I could smell Jesus approaching the white crystal gate. Oh, so sweet, my Jesus, my King is coming! I waited for Him between the two angels, my heart pounding as He drew near. One of the angels nudged me forward as if saying, "He wants you." These beautiful white angels had wings of sapphire and gold. They dressed in the most beautiful lavender robes that sparkled with fire. They too could sense Jesus coming; I could tell by the flutter of their wings. I took a deep breath as the gate opened and my best friend entered His garden.

The angels bowed at His coming, and I looked into His eyes. He received the angels' worship and then gazed at me. His blue eyes of love captivated me and drew me into His world where I am the center of His heart. I took a deep breath as sweet smells invaded my nose. I could smell frankincense and roses as He walked on the diamond path toward me. I didn't care about anything other than being with Him. He has that effect on you. You will always love Him, and He is so good at sweeping you away with Him just by one glance.

Jesus is living light, a light that no one can create or imitate. He's the most precious crystal in every realm created. Jesus is the master of beauty; our Lord is the master of pleasure. He is light manifested right before your eyes. All glory and honor belong to the living God. He is more radiant than a thousand stars. His countenance is joy, love, peace, kindness, and gentleness, and He gleams with golden light like the setting sun. Jesus, we worship you!

Every step He took toward me emitted colors mingled with gentle spirits of life! I wanted to cry, I wanted to laugh, but before I knew it, He was standing right in front of me. His overwhelming glory fell upon me as He held my hands. He smiled and waited just for a moment. Jesus is never in a rush; He enjoys patience. When He was ready, He asked me, "Son, may I have some of your time?" I was so happy I didn't even know how to answer, but He waited for me to voice my desire. "Yes, Jesus, please!"

He smiled, "Every moment with you is greater than a thousand lifetimes, Micah. Every moment with you is a gift my Father promised me. It doesn't matter what you have done. I long for these moments. I dreamt about them in my heart. You are greater than any dream spoken: you are an expression of my heart manifested to anyone who looks upon you!" He pulled me closer so that my hands would rest on His heart. He said, "Can you hear it, Micah? The very rhythm of my heart has created music to which we can dance."

As I did this, colors from inside Him spiraled out and circled us. Jesus then placed His hands on top of mine, and we spun around and around in the dancing light. I noticed we had left the ground and entered a realm of beauty that I had not seen before. Jesus said, "The most beautiful of my creation is you, son. I have given all of myself to you. I humbly ask for everything from you." Again, He waited for my answer.

"Yes, Jesus. Please take everything. I love you very much." We began to spin faster and faster until suddenly we stopped upon the sea of glass. Towering over us in indescribable light and fire was our heavenly Father. Father was so happy to see Jesus and me that He kissed us with fatherly blessings. Our Father was like a living rainbow, like a river of fire rushing up and down His being. I could see an innumerable count of angels flying around God like billowing clouds in the sky.

Our Father said to Jesus, "I am pleased, my Son, with whom you have chosen." Then He looked at me and said, "I am pleased with you, child. In my heart, a river of joy flows over your name, and I am glad! I am pleased with you, Micah, my son of light."[5]

Jesus said, as He held my hand, "Tell my church, I am ready to dance. I am ready to see my dreams come true. Only my church can fulfill this dream; I have chosen you! Come and dance with me into beauty!"[6]

Prayer: Father, I thank you for Jesus! I receive His love for me. Jesus, you have all my heart. Take me into your arms, Lord. I welcome your light and your power. I surrender to you! I want to dance with you to the song in your heart. I ask for the fire of your love to burn in me! I am receiving fire right now! Holy Spirit, open my eyes to see Jesus and the Father! I want to see my family! I love you! Holy Spirit, help me to think outside the box, help me to think the way you think! I ask to see Jesus' dreams! I ask to feel the Father's gladness!

The Beauty of Holy Spirit

This is the last writing in the Beauty of God series which is a set of visitations I had received from the Father. Understand that these visitations are not made up but are orchestrated by Father to help build up and edify the church. I ask that you pray before you read this next encounter! Ask Holy Spirit to open your imagination to engage with Him.

"Stand up!" a voice said to me in my room. My hands were on fire, and I could see angels around me, but the voice did not come from them. Again, I heard it. "Stand up now," the voice commanded me. I managed to get myself up from my bed; the presence of God was very tangible. While I stood up with my hands open to receive, a pillar of fire materialized in the room. The sounds of rushing wind and violent, crackling fire filled the atmosphere, and the angels spun around me creating a ring of light. Holy Spirit had now entered the room.[7]

"Step forward, Micah." I obeyed Him to enter the fiery funnel of holy light. Blue, green, orange, and red fire swirled around me burning my body as Holy Spirit declared, "I am here to remind you that you are not made to dwell in darkness but in the fiery passion of God. I am that passion. Walk now in purity, Micah. Walk now in holiness." I felt heat on me so intensely as the fire of God moved all around me. I was swaying back and forth by His awesome presence! I kept my hands out because I was so hungry for more of Holy Spirit. I did not want anything else, only Him!

"Look down, Micah." I obeyed, and I saw that I was standing on coals of fire. Then blazing hands of light touched my head, and Holy Spirit said, "The path of purity is the way of love. The way of holiness is the path of love. Walking in holiness is living in the Spirit, for the Spirit is love. I have come to remind you that I am the passion of God empowering you to walk in my light. I am the burning passion of God reminding you to walk in righteousness." Then a face appeared from within this tornado of fire. His head was as hot as the coals on which I was standing, and He blew fire on my face. He was burning like bronze metal with eyes like a jasper stone. I could see precious stones in His complexion that were charged with lightning! I was so overwhelmed by His power! He is power and He lives inside me. He lives inside you![8]

Holy Spirit declared, "Blessed is the pure of heart for they shall see God. They shall walk in beauty and power unhindered by the pleasures of the world. Blessed are they who walk among the coals of fire. They walk into where the enemy cannot harm them." Holy Spirit paused to let me reflect on His words then commanded, "Pick up the stones and eat." I obeyed! As I held the stone in my hand, the flames wrapped around my wrists and around my feet. Holy Spirit said, "Be prudent in speech, Micah; learn to live in beauty with your words, son.₉ Curse not what I have given life."

I consumed the stone, and it tasted like bread, and I felt waves of love move all around me. Holy Spirit now had become calm like a gentle breeze on a peaceful spring day. He held my hands and said, "I love you, Micah. I want to walk with you every day. It is my pleasure to guide you into the light of my presence. Welcome to the beauty of God." Then everything disappeared, and I was standing in my room with the angels dashing in the air.

The angel said to me, "Purity is a blessing, is it not?"

"Purity is beauty," another said.

"What do you think it means to walk in beauty, Micah?" The angels laughed and then stood still watching me with their curious blue eyes.

₁ A description of the throne room (throne of God, crystal sea, emerald rainbow…) is in Revelation 4.

₂ "Before I formed you in the womb I knew you, before you were born, I set you apart…." (Jeremiah 1:5, NIV)

₃ "The Lord is gracious and merciful, slow to anger and abounding in steadfast love." (Psalm 145:8, ESV)

4 "and to know the love of Christ that surpasses knowledge, that you may be filled with all the fullness of God." (Ephesians 3:19, ESV)

5 "While you have the light, believe in the light, that you may become sons of light." (John 12:36, ESV)

6 "The Lord your God is with you, the Mighty Warrior who saves. He will take great delight in you; in His love He will no longer rebuke you but will rejoice over you with singing." Note: the Hebrew word can also be translated as dancing. (Zephaniah 3:17, NIV)

7 "And suddenly there came from heaven a sound like a mighty rushing wind, and it filled the entire house where they were sitting. And divided tongues as of fire appeared to them and rested on each one of them. And they were all filled with the Holy Spirit." (Acts 2: 2–4, ESV)

8 "But the fruit of the Spirit is love, joy, peace, patience, kindness, goodness, faithfulness, gentleness, self-control;" (Galatians 5:22–23, ESV), and "Do you not know that you are God's temple and that God's Spirit dwells in you?" (1 Corinthians 3:16, ESV)

9 "Then one of the seraphim flew to me, having in his hand a burning coal that he had taken with tongs from the altar. And he touched my mouth and said: "Behold, this has touched your lips; your guilt is taken away, and your sin atoned for." (Isaiah 6:6–7, ESV)

Chapter 4

Finding a Friend

Chapter Outline:

- Come Back! I Will Love You!
- The Path of Light
- Having Your Own Encounters

Come Back! I Will Love You!

From the depths, my soul cried out for the living God. I waited for Him under the white rose trees. They bloom because of the waves of love coming from my heart. As each petal drops, I am left with a memory of our last meeting. Could He possibly come again as I wait for Him in His garden?

Behind me, the gate opened, and my heart reached for Him as He approached. Tears flowed from my eyes… Lord Jesus had come! I released a deep sigh. There just weren't any words—I felt so much love that I couldn't utter them. It was too deep. He stood behind me and gently placed His face next to mine while His right arm held me close. He whispered to me, "Oh how I long for the coming day, Micah. Under the rising glory of our Father, over the galaxies that sing below, you and I will please Father with my joy upon you!" He turned me around to face Him. I saw in His eyes pure and unwavering love for me. He knew every part of me. "I love you, my friend. My beautiful son of light. My glory has rested upon you, and there is no darkness in you. From the day you spoke my name before Father, your heart belonged to me and on this day, I have come to ask you…" He paused as His eyes filled up with tears, "Will you join me as my friend and never let me go?" He began to weep! Jesus rested His face in my hands… I felt His tears. He could barely utter a word. Lord Jesus, the Desire of All Nations could barely speak. I did not know what to do but hold Him. He slowly raised His blue eyes and said, "There is coming a day when my friends will leave me for another. Even some who have stood before me will be tricked by Satan's lies and leave me. I will always love them." His voice shook, "And my heart will break when they choose him over me."[1]

I was so undone by this! I had never considered how Jesus would feel about people leaving Him. He too has lost friends. He does not cry because of insecurity or shame. He cries because He remembers the day that He first held their spirit in His hand. He remembers the day when they first looked into His eyes! He saw them dancing with Him in His heart; it is beyond all knowledge and understanding! His Father had planned the wedding for His bride, and it saddens Him to know that some will not be there with Him on that day.

I didn't know what to say, "Lord, I am so weak! I have left you so many times for other pleasures. I am sorry." I kissed His head.

Jesus firmly placed His hands on my shoulders to encourage me, "I am not afraid of weakness, Micah; you shouldn't be either. Tell my people that my joy is with them, and my strength is with them. I hold them close in their times of greatest need." His voice began to shake from raw emotion,

"Tell them… I want them! I have chosen them, and I will never change my mind."

He disappeared. I was alone in the garden with the rose trees. They had now turned deep red in response to the Lord's emotion. They could feel Him too.

"Jesus come back…" I whispered, "Come back."

Then a voice spoke from among the trees, and I still don't know who it was. "This is how He feels when you leave His presence. In His heart, He waits and calls you back to Him! He is saying to those who have walked away, 'Come back, come back.'"

I could feel those people and fell to my knees. With my eyes closed, I cried out to those who have left Him, "Come back! Jesus wants you! Come back!"

Suddenly the Lord appeared next to me with His head tilted back, crying out from the deepest part of His heart. It was a cry that I cannot explain. He was interceding for them… so deep and powerful![2] Then He shouted with an intensity I have never heard before, "Come back! I will love you! Come back!"

The Path of Light

When the light faded away, I was standing on a clear path that shimmered with its own golden light. I had seen this path before. Usually, when there are pressing matters on my heart, I come here to speak with Jesus; it's a very intimate place. White oak trees that tower above me are aligned on the road leading into the rainbow presence of my heavenly Father. All paths in Heaven lead to the Father. As I prepared for the journey toward Father's glorious presence, I looked for my companion, my best friend.

A gentle breeze brushed behind my back, ushering in the presence I know so well. Jesus, my very best friend and King stood behind me and held me in His arms. He gently kissed my right ear and then breathed on the back of my head.

I giggled; I am always so captivated by Him that even the questions I have burning in my heart fade away. He is the answer to every question, but still, He intimately wants to hear what I am feeling.

Jesus came around to face me, smiling, "Son, you called for me." As Jesus stepped closer, I noticed the delightful scent of His breath, which always smells like raisins or apples. He asked, "What do you need?"

I looked into those eyes of love wondering what it was that I needed from Him. He said I had called for Him, but I did not remember why. "Jesus, I don't know what I wanted, but I know how I am feeling."

Jesus chuckled, "Walk with me and tell me how you are feeling, Micah." Jesus loves to be close to us as He is the definition of intimacy! What intimacy looks like is found in Him. He held my hand as we walked down the path under the oak trees. Heaven always responds to His presence. Even the trees swayed their branches, letting loose their white leaves to fall around us—what an enchanting moment.

Jesus waited for me to express my feelings, "Lord, today I am battling a feeling of abandonment. I didn't realize I called you. I was feeling a bit unchosen or not good enough. I know I am good enough for you, but I feel like I am not good enough for others on the earth."₃

Jesus didn't answer quickly. I love that about Him. Instead, He just tightened His hand grip as we walked. I suspect He was feeling my heart. His countenance changed from love to that of a warrior, as if He was ready to kill something for harming a loved one.

After some time, Jesus said, "Who told you that?" His voice was intense now. He looked at me, "Who told you that, Micah?" When I looked into His eyes again, they were full of fire. Jesus asked once more, "Who told you this, Micah?"

I asked, "Jesus, are you angry?"

Jesus turned away, "I am angry! I am angry at this lie spewed on you. I am angry at the one who deceived you. He is your greatest enemy. My anger is toward the enemy–Satan." Jesus looked at me fiercely, "Answer my question. Who told you this?"

I responded, "Satan did." After answering Jesus' question, I felt lighter.

Jesus said, "I would never say that you are abandoned or forgotten.₄ That thought did not originate with you either, Micah. Satan is abandoned, lost, and unwanted. He has no part of my kingdom or me. I created you for family, purpose, and completion. I am those things, Micah."

Jesus turned to me, and the fire in His eyes dimmed to a soft glimmer. His voice was gentle again as He repeated, "That lie is not part of you, son. You have a family and a purpose, and without you the world would be missing a beautiful gift."[5]

We stopped walking, and to my surprise, we were in front of our Father! The rainbows washed off His countenance onto Jesus and me. Father's glory is brighter than millions of stars. His presence is beyond the rays of the sun. As the beams of light touched Jesus and me, I looked toward the Father's heart to see a blazing column of fire! It was wild love for me, and I knew that no matter how many lies I chose to accept, they cannot remain in the presence of real love. If I believe a lie, it's because I choose to believe it. The great love of God banishes every lie![6]

Having Your Own Encounters

Intimacy with God requires consistency. That's all it takes. You just need to show up. How do we practice being consistent in our intimacy with God? These are three values I always practice and keep strong.

1) Value your time with Him. Life is full of change, and that's not bad. God loves seasons; what matters is how you live each season with Him. Value Him in every season. Change is good; new things are good. How can you embrace Him in this new season?

2) Allow yourself to do nothing when you spend time with Him. It's ok to sit with God and do nothing. Just rest with Him; be still. He just wants you.[7] As long as you give Him your heart, you are good.

3) Remember that our words matter, in prayer and outside of prayer. What escapes your lips affects the

atmosphere around you.[8] If you constantly discourage yourself, you need to let go of a lie.

God wants to connect with you. Just show up.

[1] "Those who trust in the Son possess eternal life; those who don't obey the Son will not see life." (John 3:36, TPT)

[2] "Christ Jesus is the one who died—more than that, who was raised—who is at the right hand of God, who indeed is interceding for us." (Romans 8:34, ESV)

[3] "The Lord is my helper; I will not fear; what can man do to me?" (Hebrews 13:6, ESV)

[4] "I will never leave you nor forsake you." (Hebrews 13:5, ESV)

[5] "For we are God's handiwork, created in Christ Jesus to do good works, which God prepared in advance for us to do." (Ephesians 2:10, ESV)

[6] "...perfect love casts out fear." (I John 4:18, ESV)

[7] "Draw near to God, and He will draw near to you." (James 4:8, ESV)

[8] "...out of the abundance of the heart the mouth speaks. The good person out of his good treasure brings forth good, and the evil person out of his evil treasure brings forth evil." (Matthew 12:34–35, ESV)

Chapter 5

Knowing the Father

Chapter Outline:

Beyond Perfection

This is a very recent encounter I had with Father God. By that I mean it's still very tender. Father asked me to write this for those of you who want to see what He is like and what He thinks of you. In Father's mind, you are so much more than you believe.

Father held my hand and said, "I am so proud of you, Micah. I have always been proud of you." I looked up toward His face, into the bright light to watch Him smile at me. His hair was pure radiant light and His crown of eternal glory rested on His brow. Father's robe emitted blazing flashes of light as if the garment held the power of a storm. He gently squeezed my hand, "Micah, continue to make good decisions, be honest, do what you can, and I will fill in the rest. I know you can make good decisions; I trust you, son. I am always right behind you; take the first step and I will follow."

I was shocked to hear Him say that to me. "You trust me?" Something in me broke and I started to cry. I felt so empowered, so valued.

Father knelt on one knee and placed both hands on my shoulders, looking me in the eyes. "This is sonship, Micah. Decide what you would like to do and walk forward. I am always behind you. So often you ask for guidance. I will guide you when you need it, but you don't need as much as you ask. You are wise, just like me." Father laughed slightly, "My wisdom runs in you; let it guide you.[1] If you make the wrong choice, I won't be disappointed; I am proud to call you my son. I will help you."

"But Father, I am not perfect."

He tenderly held my head between His hands, saying, "I asked you to be my son, not to be perfect. Sonship is beyond perfection."[2]

The Kindness of God

"Welcome, Micah," the golden angel said as he escorted me into the throne room. It was very peaceful there. A gentle breeze touched my face as I walked forward into the indescribable light.

Father is light and truly the master of all light. He sings His power before you. It sounds like a symphony of wind instruments giving the light that flows from His throne music with which to dance. The appearance of God is powerful: a "suddenly" like lightning when it strikes the ground. The appearance of God is illuminating, like when lightning flashes across the sky. His complexion is like diamonds that hold an inward flame. And His covering is a thousand emeralds beaming above Him like the northern lights.

The green rainbow that circles Him draws you near; it touches your heart to want to be close to Him.

Father's eyes are kind. Even though fire is coming from them, He looks at you with kindness that breaks every boundary between you and Him.

Father is love.[3]

As I walked on the crystal ocean and in between the symphony of lights dancing to His song of power, I could see the joy of my coming sweep over His face. Father truly loves me!

I reached up to Father as a child would to their parent, and He held me close to His chest while rocking me from side to side. I could feel His stomach fill with air every time He breathed.

I started to fall asleep on Father's chest. My mind was calm; my muscles relaxed as His hands softly caressed my back.[4]

He said, "Tell my children that I command all anxiety to leave their bodies. I am not struggling with their problems; it is my joy to help them, to be with them, and to heal them. My love is perfect; my kindness is perfect. I will take care of everything. I will provide what their heart needs.[5] They can come to me, and I will hold them in my arms however long they need.

The Hand of God

This is one in a series of powerful visitations about the hand of God and the wonders He has made. My goal in this is for you to be captured by His beauty; may your heart find movement in Him!

I felt the rush… the pull to come up into the eternal realm, my sight opened to see the hand of God holding light like fluttering butterflies. I rested on my bed as the spirit world began to open to me.

Angels, mighty in strength, circled and watched me, knowing that I was about to depart. As quickly as I could blink, the hand of God picked me up and carried me into His world!

I was no longer in my earthly world but flying in the spirit through time and space into His glorious reality! As we passed through the created dimensions, Father looked at me with eyes of fire. I could see the cosmos around His head like a crown, His hair shining with brilliant light! His very countenance was lightning. As God looked down at me, lightning bolts moved up and down His cheeks! His intensity was incomparable! His chest carried a living rainbow that spread outward, touching every living created being!

I rested in His hand and could feel everything: the comfort, the peace, the love which swallowed me up into His joy. I was all He wanted, just me! My eyes turned to the worlds flying past us and the moving stars around His head. I heard a voice speak, "The heavens declare the glory of God. What can compare to the mighty handiwork of God?[6] For by His hand, the worlds were made and unmade." I began to tremble at those words, however, Father's eyes never left me. He had such joy!

Finally, we stopped moving. Such wonder surrounded me that I don't know how to describe it to you. My words fail me. I had never seen such beauty. I could see everything, even the growing expanse of Heaven. It was like we were outside Heaven, and I could see the world called Heaven coming from within the Father! I was in awe! Everything I saw was made by His hand, and He still takes care of it.[7] I saw our tiny galaxy. I saw millions of other places I had never seen before, and all of them served Him. I saw the formation of equations above His head like those you would see on a whiteboard in a science lab. I saw divine wisdom coming out of His mind and interacting with all that He has made.

When I noticed Father's left hand opening to release lightning, I looked around me and saw power striking every mark! Without effort, Father circled His hand among the realms, and they began to spin and sing to Him. By the command of His hand, each world grew into a more excellent life, and His voice held each one together.

Father looked at me and said, "Who can compare to my strength? Who can measure my power? Even Heaven cannot contain me! My eyes are on you, son. I desire to show My wonders to all who wish to see my glory! You know, these realms are like the flowers in my garden, and every finished realm is under my leadership and authority. Can the enemy do this? Can he stand up to me? Can he measure my power? All these I have created with my hand, child, and by my will, I could destroy them. I am the one who names the great realms and kingdoms of Heaven. I am the one who gives authority and takes it away. Can the enemy truly give authority, Micah?

I have brought you here so that you may be confident that I am All. I AM!

As He said this, I saw power coming out of Him in waves that touched everything He made! The dimensions moved the way the flowers of the field move when wind brushes against them. I melted into my Father's hand saying, "No one is like you, Father. You are Almighty! You are unmatched!"

Father shouted, "I am! I am! I am He who breathes into the worlds made by my hand! I am the One who sits enthroned upon Heaven and I am the One who rests my feet on the earth!" He called to all the realms, "Who can match me?" And no one answered Him!

His eyes turned back to me, "The enemy's kingdom has been defeated, son.[8] Do not be afraid!"

After God said this, I trembled in His hand, but I was not afraid. I was where I was supposed to be! I saw a storm cloud form in front of me. In Almighty God's hand, a Spirit containing the full measure of His power commanded, "Lift up your heart, and hear what I have to say."

[1] "For the Lord gives wisdom; from His mouth come knowledge and understanding" (Proverbs 2:5, ESV)

[2] "See what kind of love the Father has given to us, that we should be called children of God." (1 John 3:1, ESV)

[3] "God is love." (1 John 4:8, ESV)

[4] "And He took them (the children) in His arms and blessed them, laying His hands on them." (Mark 10:16, ESV)

[5]"... do not be anxious about anything, but in everything by prayer and supplication with thanksgiving let your requests be made known to God." and Matthew 11:28, ESV, "Come to me, all who labor and are heavy laden, and I will give you rest." (Philippians 4:6, ESV)

[6]"The heavens declare the glory of God, and the sky above proclaims His handiwork." (Psalm 19:1, ESV), and "For who in the skies can be compared to the Lord? Who among the heavenly beings is like the Lord?" (Psalm 89:6, ESV)

[7]"all things were created through Him and for him. And He is before all things, and in Him all things hold together." (Colossians 1:16–17, ESV)

[8]"The reason the Son of God appeared was to destroy the works of the devil." (1 John 3:8, ESV)

Chapter 6

Imagining with God

The Imagination

It all began when a beautiful angel appeared before me. He carried Father's kindness and gentleness as he spoke to me. This beautiful messenger from Heaven had short white hair and dazzling wings! He sat down next to me with a smile and then said, "What you see in your imagination will become your reality. If you learn to see your Father with the eyes of your heart, His world will become your world."

Wow, Let's unpack this a little bit.

The imagination is what we use to interact with the spiritual and natural realms. With it, we can become what we are seeing. If we use our imagination correctly, our reality will become more and more like the truth of God's reality. What we see our Father doing becomes real.

The imagination allows us to move beyond time. It is the only thing other than your spirit that lives in two realms: the natural, which is affected by time, and the supernatural, which is beyond earthly time. What you see in your mind has the power to shape what you do. It shapes your actions. The more you "see" light or darkness in your imagination, the more significant that power is over you. You become what you see, which is why renewing the mind (Romans 12:2) is so important.

"For as he thinks within himself, so he is." (Proverbs 23:7, NASB 1995) Since our imaginations can shape so much of how we live, I believe we must sanctify our imagination and not let it become a tool for the enemy.

Ways to Keep Your Imagination Clean

Remember, what goes into your soul, the mouth will speak! The secrets hidden in your heart will be revealed through your words.

Jesus said that out of the heart the mouth speaks.[1] It is our choice to fill our souls with light. Our inward temple must be filled with light. The power of the Holy Spirit is working inside us so that we may become more like Jesus in our hearts because our actions will follow.[2] Our hearts are continually being regenerated into the glory of God.

"Now the Lord is the Spirit, and where the Spirit of the Lord is, there is liberty. But we all, with unveiled faces, beholding as in a mirror the glory of the Lord, are being transformed into the same image from glory to glory, just as from the Lord, the Spirit." (2 Corinthians 3:17–18, NASB 1995)

It is my conclusion that if we can choose to agree with Holy Spirit's power of transformation in our lives, then we can also choose to disagree with Him and allow darkness to rule in our mind and spirit. Therefore, we must set our attention higher than this world.₃ We must think about what is glorious.

> "Finally, brethren, whatever is true, whatever is honorable, whatever is right, whatever is pure, whatever is lovely, whatever is of good repute, if there is any excellence and if anything is worthy of praise, dwell on these things." (Philippians 4:8, NASB 1995)

We are all called to walk a life of holiness and purity in our thoughts. The imagination can guide your actions by the power of the Holy Spirit. Do not let darkness reign in your heart. Paul prayed that we would be filled with the spirit of wisdom and revelation and that our hearts would be enlightened.

> "That the God of our Lord Jesus Christ, the Father of glory, may give to you a spirit of wisdom and of revelation in the knowledge of Him. I pray that the eyes of your heart may be enlightened so that you will know what is the hope of His calling…" (Ephesians 1:17–18, NASB 1995)

If I were to create my own paraphrase of Ephesians 1:18, it would be that you may be filled with revelatory light! May His light from around the throne strike your heart so that you may see Him in all the glory that He desires to show you! Jesus asked that we see Him in the fullness of His glory.₄ The imagination is an easy tool for God to use to help us receive revelation.

> "Do not be conformed to this world, but be transformed by the renewal of your mind…" (Romans 12:2, NASB 1995)

What does it mean to renew? To renew your mind, you must not be molded into the patterns of this world. Your imagination must be set apart for Him. Mixing it with darkness will only result in a skewed imagination. Renewing your mind opens room for God to speak to you in a greater capacity in dreams and visions.

So, I ask you, what do you have your mind set on? What is your vision for your future? Where does your heart truly belong? The imagination is a bridge to achieving your greatest potential in life.

Choosing Light or Darkness

Sometimes we dislike the idea of things being black and white, but there is a need for that in the kingdom of God. Satan is in complete darkness, void of any form of light. What's in his "DNA" will only lead to death. What the enemy wants us to think is that there are gray areas that we can live in and still be effective in the kingdom of God. You may ask why the enemy does this. Well, he is afraid of your power to choose. You can decide who has the upper hand when it comes to choosing light or darkness; you will always have the power to choose.

But what does it mean for you to choose light when it comes to your imagination? Remember every word that God has spoken over you and think about those things. Take a moment to reflect on the promises God has spoken over you. Choose by your will to set your mind on what He (God) likes! Anything void of His light is of the enemy. Remember that you can choose by act of your will, to either think about things that are of the Father's character or of the enemy's character.

Activation Part 1: Take some time with the Father today and perform this exercise with your imagination. While you are with God, picture Him with your imagination. What does He look like to you? Take it slow, don't move too quickly. With your mind, imagine Father smiling at you. Did you know that your greatest future is with Him? Your reward is Him. Rest while looking at His face! Some will see His eyes; some will have only a feeling. Some will only see light. This is all the beginning of your reality shaping into His.

Activation Part 2: What area of your imagination have you given to sin? It can be lust, unbelief, doubt, gossip, or pride. It can be anything that does not honor Father. Ask Holy Spirit to help you renew your mind and take notes on what He reveals to you. Remember, your heart is being renewed all the time, and it is Holy Spirit's enjoyment to make you more like Jesus.

The Secret: One Million Universes

In a clearing outside of heaven, Jesus wrapped His arms around me, and we watched Father gather and unite all of the created universes that serve Him into His being.

I could see small streams of water connecting the worlds as if they were veins carrying blood that joined to the heart of Father who was immense and knew each one intimately.[5]

Father's appearance was beyond my ability to fully describe but imagine someone massive who holds the entirety of all that He has made inside Himself. He contained all the wisdom of all the worlds, and none could exist without Him.

Jesus held me close to Him, "Let us slow down for a moment, son, to observe Father taking care of the universe you see before you." Jesus gestured that we take a small canoe ride down the river that connected the worlds inside God, the Father. Jesus stepped into the canoe and helped me sit first, then He sat down and led the way down the river. We passed realms that looked like the most brilliant stars.

Jesus said to me, "What you see here is their universe. Each realm connects to the Father; not one is unknown to Him. His life is like this river that flows into each universe. He is like a living tree: the branches that extend are His wisdom, for He upholds them all, speaks to them all, and sustains them all."[6] Jesus steered the canoe on the river moving up from Father's right hand and into His shoulders down to His heart, the center.

We stopped in the heart of God, which was our universe. The most brilliant of all worlds that are connected to God our Father is the brightest light right upon His chest.

I pointed at the light, which was our universe, "This is us?" Through my laughing and crying all at once, I said, "We are His heart?"

Jesus leaned forward and held my hands, "Yes, you are in the middle above His heart. Eden. The prize of all creation, son." He smiled at me tenderly. "Does this startle you?"

"How is this possible?" I said, while Jesus gently wiped the tears from my face, "How is this possible? How am I here but there?" I didn't even know how to ask Him a question.

Jesus laughed, widening His eyes as if it was some deep secret, "Oh, do you believe in magic? Where I am, so you will also be. It is the mystical union, Micah." (To be clear, Jesus doesn't practice "magic." He was playing with me.) We laughed while He gazed into my eyes, continuing to wipe my tears away, "One of my favorite things about you, Micah, is watching you try to figure it out. You are seated with me in heavenly places.⁷ I am in you, and you are in me." He took a stone out of His pocket and showed it to me. Then He made it disappear out of His hand, "Did you see that?" He gasped, "Where did it go?" He then reached behind my ear and made the stone reappear. "There it is!" He giggled. "See...."

"Ha-ha, Jesus," I tilted my head to the side, "You got me... I love your 'magic' trick. Are you going to pull a rabbit out of a hat next?"

Jesus laughed, "I have lots of tricks, Micah." He poked my nose, "Keep watching!" We were silent, looking at each other for a moment, mesmerized by each other's beauty, until He broke the silence while reaching for my hand, "Keep watch, Micah. I will do things differently from what you may be used to doing. Just know that you are always the center of Our hearts; you are Eden, the Holy Place where God dwells.⁸ Our Father, who holds all the universes within Himself, knows everything about you. He is like the tree that holds all worlds as its leaves, but you live in the center. Keep watch."

Jesus placed His right hand on top of my left hand, leaving a white stone in my hand.

I whispered back to Him with a big smile, "Ok."

---

¹ "The good person out of the good treasure of his heart produces good, and the evil person out of his evil treasure produces evil, for

out of the abundance of the heart his mouth speaks." (Luke 6:45, ESV)

[2] "Again Jesus spoke to them, saying, "I am the light of the world. Whoever follows me will not walk in darkness but will have the light of life." (John 8:12, ESV)

[3] "...look not to the things that are seen but to the things that are unseen. For the things that are seen are transient, but the things that are unseen are eternal." (2 Corinthians 4:18, ESV)

[4] "Father, I desire that they also, whom you have given me, may be with me where I am, to see my glory that you have given me because you loved me before the foundation of the world." (John 17:24, ESV)

[5] "And God said, "Let there be an expanse in the midst of the waters, and let it separate the waters from the waters." And God made the expanse and separated the waters that were under the expanse from the waters that were above the expanse. And it was so. And God called the expanse Heaven." (Genesis 1:6-8, ESV)

[6] "And He is before all things, and in Him all things hold together." (Colossians 1:17, ESV)

[7] "But God, being rich in mercy, because of the great love with which He loved us, even when we were dead in our trespasses, made us alive together with Christ—by grace you have been saved—and raised us up with Him and seated us with Him in the heavenly places in Christ Jesus." (Ephesians 2: 4–6, ESV)

[8] "Know that the Lord is God. It is He who made us, and we are his; we are His people, the sheep of His pasture." (Psalm 100:3, ESV)

Chapter 7

Maturing in the Prophetic

Chapter Outline:

- Love the Gift You Have
- The Family Table
- Finding Community
- Practicing Obedience at the Store
- Going to the Movies

Love the Gift You Have

What do I do when people don't believe me? Simple, I go to another apple. Not everyone is my apple to pick. That's okay. The last thing I want to do is argue with people.

Some people think that I am crazy, and honestly, I get it. I truly do. I am never mad when someone thinks I am crazy. There are times when I think, *Lord... seriously?*

My goal is not the visions, the dreams, or the visitations... my goal is to create a culture of friends for Jesus. I want those who read my writings to become who they are created to be. Don't get me wrong: I LOVE my supernatural encounters. God made me this way and put me on Earth for a reason.

I am a Seer. Not everyone is, and that's good!

A Seer is different from someone who has visions. You can have visions and not be a Seer; it's possible. More on that another time.

Many people want visions or to see into the spirit realm but they don't want to be a Seer. Honestly, being a Seer is not for everyone, just like being a Pastor is not for everyone. Everyone can prophesy, but not all can be a Prophet. Everyone can preach, but not all are Pastors.[1]

I want to talk about the elephant in the room here. Folks, it's okay to ask God for more, but sometimes you may not get it right now, or you may never get the gift for which you have been asking. You may have been asking for visitations or angelic encounters, but nothing has happened. You must be okay that it may never happen, and you must not allow the enemy to steal the gifts that God has given you.

You have gifts already that you must steward and cultivate. You have a chocolate chip cookie on your plate, and yet you are screaming for a snickerdoodle. Some of you are so distracted by another's gifts that you're losing your own.

We must learn to value what we have. Why would God answer your plea for another gift when you can't be thankful for what you have? God will NOT give a gift to a stingy, whining heart. I know this because I have been there.

He will not give it, and He may never give it to you out of His wisdom. It's not that He loves you less.

Yes, Father gives good gifts![2] Yes, ask and desire more gifts, but what about what you have already?

Do not ask for gifts out of a lack of identity. This is why your identity must be in Christ. The reality is that Father may say "no", is saying "no", or may be saying "not right now". And you must be okay with that and trust His answer.[3] You must be firm in His love! Know that His "no" is not hate; it's wisdom and it is love.

So, to summarize my random thoughts, not everyone is your apple. Suppose people think you are crazy; it's not the end of the world. You probably do sound crazy. Jesus did. Have you read the Bible lately? Some of you are an apple tree trying to be a pear tree. You can want to be something else, but the fact is, you are who you are. Some of you are Evangelists trying to be a Pastor, or a Teacher trying to be a Prophet. Just be who you are. Eat your chocolate chip cookie and be thankful. Who knows, maybe you will get a snickerdoodle later, but enjoy what you have been given. Father doesn't give gifts to stingy, whining children.

Learn to love what you have!

The Family Table

Prophets and those with prophetic voices, did you know that the glory of God will not come at its full capacity unless you come home? Your prophetic words about God's coming glory will not be fulfilled until you return to the church, get into a community, and bring your presence and contribution to the Kingdom around believers.[4] It's the enemy's strategy to keep you out of the church, not Jesus'.

In a Holy Spirit trance, I watched a couple coming to a party of golden light, laughter, and excitement. As I watched this, Jesus appeared to me in this trance; He was among us all! He was among the laughter, the glory, and the community.

His presence was beautiful. When this couple joined the party, Jesus exclaimed, "Welcome back home, Prophets; We are so glad you are here. Now we can party. You make the whole system better; I am glad you came back home."

I know history has not been kind toward the Prophets, but that is history, not the future. Jesus wants you to leave the desert of rejection and isolation of the past. The glory of God is waiting for you to come back to the churches. The church is not waiting for your correction, your warnings, not even your prophecies. We are waiting for YOU! Just YOU! We want YOU! We want your friendship, personality, and person before your prophetic words. So come home; don't live in the past anymore.

Be quick to be a friend before being a Prophet. Be quick to laugh before you shout out the mysteries of the Kingdom. The church needs a friend first before a Prophet.[5]

You will prophesy, but you will prophesy from a place of family, not isolation! You will prophesy around the family table, not from the place of rejection. You will prophesy from friendship, love, and acceptance. You will be one with the community for which Jesus so desired and prayed in John 17.[6]

The glory of God is coming! Why is the glory delayed? The glory is waiting for the Prophets to come home, to come back to the community of believers.

Finding Community

Prophets rise from healthy prophetic cultures and communities. For a Prophet to grow, they need others to speak into their lives, to equip, and to pastor them. It is not just the lead Pastor's job to pastor Prophets; it takes a community. A healthy Prophet comes from a healthy community.[7]

I know some of you who follow me on social media do not know where you can find a healthy community. It is important to recognize that a healthy community doesn't mean a perfect one!

Some of you may be asking, "Micah, how did you find a community or local church?"

I had to let go of my ideal perfect church and learn to love. I gave up trying to fix something I could not fix. I gave up trying to give the hard words. I stopped trying to be the one with the answers from God or to be the person who shared the angelic encounter every time. I had to let it go.

What's more important was that I found a community of believers who I could love, and they could love me!

Jesus told me in a dream, "Son, your ideal church where everyone receives you and hears your words is not my church. Your ministry has nothing to do with you but with me. I judge how well you've loved and if you've had a heart to love imperfection. Stop waiting for a church to receive you perfectly and learn to love them as they will learn to love you."

Many prophetic people are looking for a perfect church to receive them, but they will not find it. Did you know that you are part of the imperfect church? That means you have to learn to love, work with, and be patient with everyone, just as they must do the same for you.

You won't get perfect until Jesus comes back. However, the journey until He comes is amazing! You get to experience grace just like everyone else. You get to be loved through your imperfections, just like everyone else. You get to be called higher, held accountable, and encouraged just like everyone else, all for the glory of the Lord.

You may be thinking to yourself these thoughts:

> "But Micah, the church is not ready for what I have to bring."

> "God called me out of the church."

> "God called me to the desert."

> "I am called to correct."

> "They weren't ready to...."

> "They don't like what I have to say."

The church… this and that… I have heard it all. Now is the time to let go of your perfect church world and learn to love the one right in front of you. When Jesus comes for His pure and spotless church, you will be among the ones who have been cleansed just like everyone else.

For those of you who feel called to correct or judge, this is what Jesus told me, "You cannot properly correct something you do not love well. Heaven knows what words you use based on your love. Father will not trust one who does not love well, and He will not send a wolf to His sheep."

The church community is waiting for you....

Practicing Obedience at the Store

One time Jesus asked me to take Him to a local department store, named Kohl's. This is what I mean when I say that the glory of the Lord is going to do incredible things. "Micah, take me to Kohl's."

"Why?" I remember asking, "Why?" I didn't want to go shopping; I didn't want anything at Kohl's. "What are you going to get at Kohl's, Jesus?"

"I'm going to go shopping."

"Shopping for what?" I asked.

"Take me to Kohl's, Micah."

I got in the car and drove to Kohl's and decided that I would buy some socks. I walked around in Kohl's and Jesus appeared there–nothing new for me, I'd seen Him before. Cool. I think I'm the only one that can see Him. We walk around having a conversation.

I got my pair of socks and went into the checkout line. I was talking to Him now in my mind because I didn't want people to think I was crazy for talking out loud. The lady scanned the socks and looked up, looked at me, and looked at Jesus. It didn't compute with me in the beginning. She said, "Who's your friend?" I said, "Who's who?"

She said, "Who's your friend?"

I looked at Him and thought, *She can't be talking about you, she can't see you.* I said, "There's no one here."

And she said, "Your friend—who is he?" and I gasped, realizing she could see Him. Now I'm a mess and I'm trying to remember all the things I learned about leading people to Jesus, and I can't even talk.

Jesus extended His hand and said to her, "I'm Jesus."

Then she straight up said to Him, "I hate you."

He started to talk to her. He told her about her life, her past, all these intimate things about her that only He would know, and she was a royal hot mess. She received Him on the spot! AND the people in the line behind me saw that. They saw that man, Jesus. People were all amazed at what was going on. The presence of God was in Kohl's and then Jesus just disappeared, out of sight, and left me standing there with those people.

Going to the Movies

God woke me up and said, "Micah, take me to go see the '*Avengers*' movie", which was *Avengers: Infinity War* playing at the theaters at the time. I'm a huge Marvel fan, so I had probably watched it at least five times before the Lord asked me to go with Him, but I had no problem going to see it again. I could watch that movie all the time. "Gladly, Jesus! You want to go and see '*Avengers*'?"

He said, "Yeah, take me to see '*Avengers*'."

"OK, yippee for me."

I went to the theater to get a ticket. I even thought, *Should I buy Him a ticket? Well, I'll just get in there and if He walks in, I'll buy Him a ticket.* These are the things that I think about. So, I got a ticket, got some pop and popcorn. The movie theater was cold, so I had my blanket and I sat down, and I enjoyed the movie.

In comes this guy. He's got his drink, has a Spider-Man t-shirt on, and sandals. Sandals with socks—white socks. So, I'm sitting there watching the movie and hear, "Hey, man, can I have some of your popcorn?"

"OK", I gave him some popcorn, thinking the whole time, *this is my popcorn*. Then he drank his pop, and we finished the movie. He got up while I was still sitting down, reflecting on the movie, and He said, "Man, what would you think if people just thought a little bit more like the superheroes? Like where are the Spider-Mans and where are the Iron Mans? Where are the Captain Americas? If people thought more like superheroes do, we'd get a whole lot done."

I said, "Absolutely! I totally agree with you. We need to think better about ourselves…." I was so fired up, I said, "My name is Micah."

He shook my hand and said, "My name is Jesus," and then He just disappeared. He left the theater. He was gone. I screamed! I tried to text my family, but my fingers were shaking.

I got in the car, and I was screaming and crying. I've seen Jesus before, but I was thinking, *He was next to me the whole time!?* I asked Holy Spirit, "How did He get in the building?" Holy Spirit started to bring to my remembrance times where in my subconscious I noticed the guy. I remember seeing Him in line to get His pop. He was there the whole time. There were people talking to Him, and they didn't even know it was Him! They were talking to Jesus! Jesus was in the building!

I was thinking, *OK, Lord, give me a scripture. Just help me out here a little bit.* He reminded me of the passage where He was walking with the disciples on the road to Emmaus and how they had no idea who He was.[8]

[1] "And He gave the apostles, the prophets, the evangelists, the shepherds and teachers, to equip the saints for the work of ministry, for building up the body of Christ" (Ephesians 4:11–12, ESV)

[2] "If you then, who are evil, know how to give good gifts to your children, how much more will your Father who is in heaven give good things to those who ask him!" (Matthew 7:11, ESV)

[3] "For my thoughts are not your thoughts, neither are your ways my ways, declares the Lord." (Isaiah 55:8, ESV)

[4] "And let us consider how to stir up one another to love and good works, not neglecting to meet together, as is the habit of some, but encouraging one another…" (Hebrews 10:24–25, ESV)

[5] "How good and pleasant it is when God's people live together in unity!" (Psalm 133:1, NIV)

[6] "that they may all be one, just as you, Father, are in me, and I in you, that they also may be in us, so that the world may believe that you have sent me. The glory that you have given me I have given to them, that they may be one even as we are one, I in them and you in me, that they may become perfectly one, so that the world may know that you sent me and loved them even as you loved me…" (From John 17, ESV)

[7] "Let the word of Christ dwell in you richly, teaching and admonishing one another in all wisdom, singing psalms and hymns

and spiritual songs, with thankfulness in your hearts to God."
(Colossians 3:16, ESV)

[8] "and they were talking with each other about all these things that
had happened. While they were talking and discussing together,
Jesus himself drew near and went with them. But their eyes were
kept from recognizing him…" (From Luke 24:13–28, ESV)

Chapter 8

Developing as a Seer

Chapter Outline:

The White Eagle: Chazah

I closed my eyes to listen to the wind rushing by me and took a deep breath of the heavenly air as my senses joined in the beauty and wonder of this realm! I knew I had arrived in Heaven, but I had not looked yet to see where I was in Heaven. Part of me wanted to be surprised.

I peeked with one eye to see where I was, and I couldn't believe it! I was high up in the trees—enormous trees of green light. I was standing in a nest made of gold. I rushed to the edge of it to get a better view of the scene. I saw clouds of light wrapping around the trees like a garment. The glory of God was shining through the morning sky as I once again took a deep breath to contain my excitement. *What was about to happen? What would I see this time?* I had so much joy! Suddenly, I heard the cry of an eagle drawing near me. I made my way to the center of the nest and looked toward the sky. Coming in my direction, at high speed, was a great, white and golden eagle. I felt so much power coming toward me as

His flight brought Him lower to the nest. It was spectacular to watch this eagle descend with His pure white wings. The eagle had intense blue eyes of fire that searched my soul. He was about eight feet tall while His wingspan was the largest that I have ever seen. He was radiant with the brightness of the setting sun! He was the Lord! The Lord in the form of a white eagle. I had seen Him this way a couple of times before through visitations. I had ridden Him around the throne room once when I was 15 and other times throughout my college career. He called Himself "Chazah".[1] He circled the large nest and cried aloud with His powerful voice.

Chazah landed with authority, and He declared, "Fly with me! I command you to fly!" I reached for His white feathered neck to embrace Him.

"When you fly with me, you will experience rest. Fly above the warfare and into the glory of God's marvelous light. It is where you belong—in the light as He is in the light. Do you know this is where the prophetic shall dwell? Eagles who live in the light rest in my nest where I feed them. You are such an eagle, Micah, not of the world below, but from above." He opened His wings and said, "Take refuge here, Micah."[2] I went under the eagle's wings to rest in His shadow when gold began to pour onto my head. He said, "Intimacy is hiding in the shade of my wing. Revelation flows upon you." I could see that the very tips of the eagle's feathers were gold, woven with the glory of God. He was Lord of the eagles—the highest of them all.

I began to hear the cry of others around me. I walked from underneath His wings to the edge of the nest to watch the fog clear. I saw golden eagles flying from tree to tree, calling to the world below them to come up higher.[3] These powerful birds never moved their wings, they just soared upon the wind.

The White Eagle said, "Some are raised in the mountains, and some are raised in the trees: two places where I raise the prophetic voices, Micah." I was amazed how they could fly so peacefully—no striving, just peace. "The prophetic is cultivated in a place of waiting in peace, Micah. My prophetic people, who will be unlike any other, will be free from anxiety, depression, fear, intimidation, and manipulation! They will be the ones giving a face to God Almighty… they will teach others how to fly to the nest and be raised in my presence, where I will feed them from my mouth. These voices will not be about accuracy, but about the image of God being manifested through them. They will have eyes like no one has seen; they will hear the thunder from the throne of God. They will fly into the face of God and come out golden!"

Chazah opened His wings once again, "Come fly with me!"

I climbed on the eagle's back, and His enormous white wings lifted us toward the sunlight. He said, "We will fly into the face of God!" Other eagles began to fly with us into the light—they followed Him! I could see that the sunlight was the glory of God pulsating abundant love from the center. Chazah said, "To see and behold your God you must stand in His face and become what you behold.[4] The mission of the prophetic voice is to see, behold, and become. Declare what you have heard! Declare what you have seen and teach others how to fly into the face of God." Then golden eagles, hundreds of them, began to cry out loud in worship to the White Eagle as we entered the face of God.

Chazah warned me, "There is no other way, Micah. It is possible to be consumed with such darkness that you become like vultures or crows. Vultures feast on the dead—demons! This can happen to those who will not give me their lives and choose not to rise in holiness. Crows are those who have let bitterness and anger enter them! Their voices have become annoying sounds of criticism and judgment. There is no love in them. There is another type of bird, Micah, that is paper eagles. They're fake; they become just an echo out of jealousy. What they have is not real, but their fame is real, and they will be tossed by the wind of adversity. They link themselves to others, forming alliances just to strengthen their own ego. Do not be like them—they are the worst. When fire comes, they will have nothing left. I can cast out demons from the vultures and I can heal the broken heart of the crows, but the pride from the paper eagles will not let me come near." Chazah sighed… "Do not become like them, Micah. Check your heart. It is easy to fool yourself if you are not walking in humility."

I buried my face in His feathers and whispered to Him, "I love you, Chazah. Forgive me for not yielding to your leadership. I want to become a golden eagle representing the face of God."

Chazah said, "Then fly with me! Come to the nest and I will feed you from my mouth. Rest under my wings when you are wounded, and I will heal you."

"He found him in a desert land, And in the howling waste of a wilderness; He encircled him, He cared for him, He guarded him as the pupil of His eye. Like an eagle that stirs up its nest, That hovers over its young, He spread His wings and caught them, He carried them on His pinions. The LORD alone guided him,

And there was no foreign god with him..."
(Deuteronomy 32:10–12, NASB 1995)

"Yet those who wait for the LORD will gain new strength; They will mount up with wings like eagles, They will run and not get tired, They will walk and not become weary." (Isaiah 40:31, NASB 1995)

The White Eagle: The Night Owls

I lifted my head once more to see our destination as we flew into the face of God. The realm of light was so breathtaking! All my senses were overloaded with imagination and destiny. Incredible, indescribable brightness welcomed me as both Chazah and I went into intimacy with God. Chazah is a depiction of Jesus. His greatest desire is that we would know God intimately and that we might find our place in His light.

Eventually, Chazah and I entered the face of God, a divine light of gold and silver! I cannot comprehend the glory of the Creator, but the One who is my true home was looking at me right in the eyes and a smile of love kissed my heart as I beheld my God.[5]

The White Eagle spoke, "Son, welcome to the face of God—the destiny of all who see and hear. This is how Moses knew God face to face—a reality deeper than the very earth he stood on. Moses knew my way and my face was revealed to him. Do not be concerned about the process of revelation; instead, be one who stands in the face of God."

We flew around the Father's wondrous glory with thousands of angels flying between us declaring His majesty! It was marvelous! Our Father, like a bright jewel, raised His hands to hold up divine light! The White Eagle said, "You will see even greater things than the things on which the angels have dared to look. All that is His He gives freely to those who are hungry for more. Micah, the prophetic is about encountering God and releasing others into that encounter. The eagles must learn to fly around the throne!" We continued our circle around Father, and around Him were also seraphim of fire, shining with purity, and cherubs with large wings hovering before Him, crying out, "Holy!"

Chazah said, "Come with me now to the river of fire." We descended to this river flowing from God, and I saw eagles, who were sullied or defiled, bathing in the fire. Some of their wings were broken and angels had to help carry them to the river of fire. Chazah landed near the riverbank and said, "These are some who have compromised, Micah. Do not live in compromise or it will cause your wings to break. Let your 'yes' be 'yes' and your 'no' be 'no'. I will send out angels to heal the wounded Prophets. If they do not become healed, they will turn into a vulture or a crow."

"Lord," I replied, "What makes paper eagles then? How does an eagle become a paper eagle?"

He answered with authority, "You shall love the Lord your God with all your heart, with all your mind, and with all your strength. You shall love me. They forget the first commandment.[6] Paper eagles care for themselves, for their impact—so much that they tag along to someone else's anointing rather than to me. You shall have no other god! Listen to me, you shall have no other god. Repent and be healed."

I felt such gravity in His words, "Lord, how do the paper eagles, vultures, and crows become healed?"

He opened His wings, "Come abide under my shadow and let my love rain down upon you! Return to your first love."

I saw vultures that were in cages being released to bathe in the river, and golden eagles were near to encourage them. The demons left the vultures, and the vultures began to grow up into eagles again. Some of the golden eagles took the previous vultures back to the nest in the mountains or trees! The crows were chained, and the angels broke their chains before putting them into the river of fire. Then the golden eagles lead them to the nest.

"Come with me! I want to show you something else." We flew to another area around the throne to encounter a group of owls. I was amazed at the appearance of these beautiful birds: they were silver and white, and some were so white that they glowed with the brightness of the Father! There must have been hundreds of them watching the throne of God.

The White Eagle said, "These are another kind of prophetic voice. They are mistaken for eagles, but they are not… I awaken them with dreams and visitations in the night. The owl sees into the night, and the eagle sees in the day. I have given the owl the ability to see the plans of the enemy — darkness shakes from the light of their wings. I raise them in barns and caves until it is time! They hear my call in the night and in dreams they receive it!"

I asked, "What are they doing here?"

Chazah opened His wings, and the owls turned toward Him to bow in worship, "They must gaze into light lest they become dark and eat the demonic realm as food. Now, behold light to keep you right!" I could see His great love for the owls, and they loved Him. The White Eagle said, "This is my prophetic company, owls who discern the enemy plans and alert the people. They must be filled with love, or they will look for evil in what I call good!"

The presence of God was all over these birds, and they stood in confidence in who they are. As I said, they were white and silver with glory! I wondered how these birds would be received within the church, these voices of the night.

Chazah said, "Do not despise the owls, Micah. All need to work together! The owl sees into the night and the eagle sees in the day!"

I noticed that not all owls were the same: some looked like great horned owls and other various types, but their feathers were all white. "Lord, why are all their feathers white?"

He answered, "Because they have chosen holiness! They walk in righteousness and the enemy hates that. They lead by example and they prophesy! They do not become like the darkness to which they are assigned. The golden eagles carry my presence, and then holiness turns their feathers gold! The owls carry my light, and their feathers turn white."

Chazah then raised His wings to fly around the throne. I rested my head on His back as the wind brushed by me. I was glad the owl and eagle got to work together to release the prophetic.

Chazah said with such peace in His voice, "Child, my golden eagle, it is time to see beyond your wildest dreams. Even the owl must take his place before me. Owls are hunters; go and hunt… bring in the lost and be my light that shines, and darkness may turn away. Live in holiness. Join with the eagles whose sight is from above, who see into dimensions that call forth repentance to the Earth. Come and be fed in my nest and I will give my voice to you."

I felt such peace with Him. While I briefly closed my eyes, I found myself returning to my room looking out my window in wonder. The portal above closed. Maybe I will come back to Chazah again…. I will fly!

Chazah Returns: The Gold Mountain

Chazah is a large beautiful white eagle with feathers dipped in gold. He is looking for a rider. Who will ride Him? Who is willing to give up compromise and fly on the back of the Lord toward the face of God? You cannot fly Him and keep your will. It must be Him alone! God dwells upon the Gold Mountain. Glory rains down on His dwelling creating rivers of shining jewels by His feet. Chazah wants to take you there; leave your way and fly!

It was a typical afternoon when the Great Eagle Chazah returned for our next flight. I was not expecting His presence, but something changed in the atmosphere. I sensed the presence of the Lord rushing when instantly my spirit shot out of my body into a brilliant portal where millions of eagles cried out to the heavenly realm. Golden eagles with illuminated wings lifted praise toward the heavens as we climbed up into the dazzling light. Beautiful melodies melted from my mouth and created ribbons crackling like fire in the wind.

We climbed higher and higher into Heaven until we peeked into the realm of divine light, the kingdom of Almighty God and His holy Son, Jesus. The eagles dashed by me toward a golden mountain to the east of Heaven, but the spirit took me to a beautiful castle made of solid diamonds.

I couldn't believe such an amazing structure existed, but then again, I was in Heaven. I noticed at the highest point of the castle some angels appeared like winged lions, protectors of the great home. Our holy God made these lions from light and crystal shards from the sea of glass! Upon my arrival, they raised their wings and roared with might! The Spirit set me in front of a massive golden door that led into the castle. On this door appeared emerald eyes by the thousand which gazed at me. The wings connected these eyes by soft glorious light. On my approach, the door swung open to a huge hall.

I ran! I ran through the great hall where angels and other creatures convened for reasons I do not know. I was looking for the Lord. I was looking for Chazah.

I cried, "Chazah. I am here!" My heart was pounding because I loved Him. I wanted to fly with Him again. Down the long hall, I searched for Him. I investigated many rooms, asking where the White Eagle rested. In these rooms were angels and strange creatures I had never seen before. One was a giant turtle with wings growing out of its shell; another was a large three-horned bird with a long beautifully feathered tail. They were speaking but I did not know the things about which they were speaking.

It began to snow soft white feathers around the company and me. The unique group who was present in this room froze in a crystal case as the power of the White Eagle's presence entered with great shafts of light. I sighed deeply and my heart began to rest. A soft wind blew away the scene around me like drifting snow. Sounds of heavenly music, unlike anything I have heard, opened my senses to receive the awesome presence of the Lord. Chazah, who is the manifest interpretation of Jesus, descended gently into the world of light. His wings stretched over me and released an aroma of spices that drew me further into His commanding presence. The snow of white feathers drifted past us in the wind as Chazah spoke.

"You searched for me! How many people search for me, child? Do they come by the drifting of the white feathers or the wind which pulls them? No, child, what you see here is the result of hunger. Hunger releases my presence. Hunger brings you into a world of light and revelation. You will not find me where the common tongue lives but by the language of the spirit." He looked down at me with piercing eyes and said, "Those who search for me will find me, and they will also find themselves in me!"[7]

"Lord, where was I before this?" I asked.

He smiled, "You were in the castle known as Destiny, child. There are many castles in the heavens. Destiny only reveals itself when there is hunger." I was so overwhelmed during this moment as the white feathers blew by us. Chazah's voice thundered, "It is time to fly now! Climb upon my back," He said as He lowered His neck to the ground so that I could climb. We quickly flew to the east where the Golden Mountains stand.

Around the Golden Mountains, the Great White Eagle led me into the face of Almighty God. The wind of angels gusted by me while Chazah's call echoed among the highest heavens, and into the great light we flew. I was not afraid; I was at home... flying high above the clouds... above the warfare into my Father's light! I could hear His wings, raising and lowering while He commanded the wind by His will. Chazah said, "Do you remember, Micah, the longing to be with your Father? The eagle's desire is for the nest of God; the feeding is about to begin, child. All who have wings fly."

I felt it. I felt the desire to be with God as we flew into His face, a world of intimacy. I sat up to breathe in the fragrance of Heaven then smiled at the flickering Starlight Angels that danced around this beautiful place. I felt peace... I did not want to leave... ever!

Chazah said, "You must go back, Micah. The face of God is for anyone who has ears to hear and eyes to see. I call to the Earth–to any person who desires intimacy with God. Fly to the nest; intimacy is about to begin. Come and be fed the food of light." We continued to soar on the wind toward the mighty mountains that harvested the glory of the Lord.

[1] Strong's Exhaustive Concordance of the Bible. (n. d). 2372 Chazah: to have a vision of—behold, look, prophesy, provide, see. Retrieved October 6, 2022, from https://biblehub.com/strongs/hebrew/2372.htm.

[2] "How precious is your steadfast love, O God! The children of mankind take refuge in the shadow of your wings." (Psalm 36:7, ESV)

[3] "For as the heavens are higher than the earth, so are my ways higher than your ways and my thoughts than your thoughts." (Isaiah 55:9, ESV)

[4] "And we all, with unveiled face, beholding the glory of the Lord, are being transformed into the same image from one degree of glory to another." (2 Corinthians 3:18, ESV)

[5] "Lord, you have always been our eternal home, our hiding place from generation to generation." (Psalm 90:1, TPT)

[6] "'Love the Lord your God with every passion of your heart, with all the energy of your being, and with every thought that is within you.' This is the great and supreme commandment." (Matthew 22:37–38, TPT)

[7] "You will seek me and find me, when you seek me with all your heart." (Jeremiah 29:13, ESV)

Chapter 9

Ministering Angels

Chapter Outline:

Why It's Important to Know about Angels

One question that I'm often asked is, "Why do you talk about angels so much?" If you want to understand why it's important to know about angels, read Hebrews 1. It describes what angels are and who they are. Hebrews 1 describes the angels' relationship with Jesus, and it describes our function. Hebrews 1:14 says that angels are "ministering spirits".

What does Hebrews 1 mean by ministering spirits? Angels are called spirits because spirits come from God.

Angels are spiritual beings that God created whose priority is to minister, or serve, directly unto God. As a result of them worshiping God and ministering unto Him first, He then sends them to minister or serve you. Angels are a gift to you.

What do angels do? Angels not only fight on your behalf or protect on your behalf, but they also are a gift. They give you what is needed for that time, for that season, for that event. God sends them from His throne, and He commands them to look after you, to watch over you. A lot of you have different assignments in your life: you are probably involved in ministry or even in the marketplace. Angels provide gifts to you and provide service to you for what is needed. For example, if you need protection, they protect you. If you need courage, they bring courage to you. If you need a companion when you are feeling sad or depressed or dealing with grief, they will be a friend to you. They bring understanding, they bring joy, and they also listen! I've had experiences where I'm talking to myself, and although the Lord hears every word I'm saying, He's not the only one in the room listening.

There was a moment when I was going through something very challenging. I would talk to myself and encourage myself and say things that were honest and open about my challenges. As I was talking, the Lord opened my eyes, and sitting next to me I saw Eden, the angel that God has assigned to me. Eden smiled and was very kind and polite. He has been a wonderful friend to me.

When I saw Eden listening to me, I was startled because I thought, "Shouldn't you be fighting something? You've got your weapons; shouldn't you be fighting something? Or do you have a message for me? Do you have something you want to say?" Eden answered, "No, what you need right now is someone to listen to you. I am being a listening ear to you."

Angels are fascinating because they are not only warriors, but they have compassion; they have the ability to understand what you're going through.

So be encouraged that you have help! You're not lacking in anything; the Lord has provided all that you need. Also, He has given you a companion from Heaven, a spiritual being and ministering spirit that has come to you to give you joy, to give courage and boldness, and to be the friend you need. Your angel is the one who listens to you when there's hardship, so you have help. A lot of the things that you think you do on your own are done with your angel's help. That angel who is receiving no credit is behind you, cheering you onward. You couldn't do things without your angel.[1]

I hope it blesses you and encourages you to thank the Lord for the ministering spirits that He has assigned to your life. Thank the Lord for the help that you receive because these angels are awesome and are good companions.

Micah, I Want to See Angels....

So, you want to see angels? Let's talk about it....

Every day I'm asked about angels. It's true, those bright-eyed, winged spirits are my friends... no, really, we are friends, but they aren't like us one bit. They are very content with not being seen because of their identity in God. Yes, angels have an identity, but they are not sons, they are only servants or ministering spirits. One of my favorite things about angels is how relational they are! When they know you've seen them, they will never leave you alone again! They love friends and they love being a part of your life.

I realize that some of my stories about angels may seem extreme or unusual, but walking in the angelic realm is normal for me and rather easy. Even while you are reading this, angels are looking over your shoulder, smiling as I talk about them. Just turn around and say, "Hello". Engaging with angels is not rocket science... nope, it's not! It is easy! All it takes is for you to think outside the box.

My goal for this moment is to help you understand who angels are and give you some ideas on how to interact with them daily.

Angels are Ministering Spirits

"Are they not all ministering spirits, sent out to render service for the sake of those who will inherit salvation?" (Hebrews 1:14, NASB 1995)

Angels are also messengers and servants of God who obey the voice of the Lord!

"Bless the Lord, you His angels,
Mighty in strength, who perform His word,
Obeying the voice of His word!" (Psalm 103:20, NASB)

Now Micah, when you say that you see angels, what does that mean?

Well, I see angels in all kinds of ways but the most common is through my physical eyes... at least it feels that way. The spirit world is so real to me that I forget there are two worlds in which I am engaging. To me, seeing angels is like looking at another person. I can see, touch, and hear them the same way I see and hear a person speaking right in front of me. Crazy, right? I thought so too until I became friends with angels.

My days look like this: I am walking through Kroger to get food, and there is an angel standing at the register minding his own business. I just glance at him because I am used to seeing angels around me, however, he responds differently. He follows me throughout the store talking to me about his job and what he did the other day.

Sometimes they will ask if we can pray together. We then pray together, what fun!

I have had angels follow me around in stores who were so big that their heads were into the ceiling!

I remember one time I was shopping for shoes when an angel came up to me and asked, "Which shoes do you like?" I responded under my breath because people were around us— I didn't want to look crazy, "I like these brown ones!" He placed his hand on his hips and said, "Good choice. Brown shoes are needed to walk in the spirit. It's humility. Do you know an easy way to see us? It's by walking in humility. Humility and faith to believe in the imagination." I looked at the angel with a smile, "Thank you for helping me buy shoes, sir." He disappeared.

There it is folks… your answer. Walk in humility and you will see more than you think. Now please understand you may not see them the same way I do, it can come in many ways.

How might you see or experience angels? Let's look!

Wind/Cool Breeze:

Have you ever felt during worship and prayer times a slight wind or breeze around you? Well sometimes it's not the air vents, it's angels. Often, angels will float about you moving their wings to stir up wind! If you feel that, take some steps in humility and faith and thank the Lord for the angels. Then ask, "Why are you here?" By the way, they can speak to your spirit because you are just as much a spirit as they are. If you were wrong and it was the air vents, you really didn't lose or miss out on anything. However, what if it was an angel and you were too busy being skeptical and missed a visitation? That's worse. Still, God will redeem every moment and give you an infinite number of chances. The truth is that angels encamp around those who fear God.

"The angel of the Lord encamps around those who fear him, and he delivers them." (Psalm 34:7, NIV)

Flashes of Light/Sparkles:

Angels can often be discerned as flashes of light in the room or sparkles that you can see floating around you. No, it is not your mind playing tricks on you. Remember, let's have a little humility and some faith here. Why the sparkles? Angels are made up of light and when you look inside their bodies you can see flashes of fire or light. Their wings have sparkles on them from the throne room, and when they move around, they leave a mess in the spirit realm. Ha! So many sparkles! Sometimes these sparkles will manifest in the natural realm and get everywhere! It's the glory realm! Angels will release the glory of God! So, when this happens, just thank God for it! Ask the Lord to show you more of His glory! He will! Angels are there because He loves you and they want you to engage with what God is doing!

I can remember one time when an angel in complete gold showed up in my bedroom. It turned the light in my room gold! He said, "Behold the glory of God! See His beauty! Pray and He will open your eyes!" He vanished but left gold dust on my hands! Whoa! More, Lord Jesus!

Hello Mr. Angel, is that you?

You can sense angels too. Ever have a moment when you are by yourself and feel someone watching you? Or you're in worship and you feel like someone just walked into the room? Well, you have a visitor! Say "Hello"! Go on now, don't be shy... I promise they won't bite! What if it's a demon? Simply tell them to leave in the name of Jesus. Don't be so afraid of the dark side that it keeps you from experiencing the power of God.

Angels are always around us. We just need to believe and walk in humility. Growing skepticism is not going to help you. You must become like a child in your heart.

There are some angels so big that they fill the entire sky. One day while driving, I saw an angel made completely of fire on a horse as big as the sky. He called himself "Flame and Glory". Angels are always ready to be a part of your life and it doesn't take a crazy Prophet to encounter them either. It just takes some faith and humility.

Imagination:

This is another easy way to see angels. Paul talks about the eyes of the heart being enlightened. The imagination is powerful and serves as a bridge to see in the spirit. We are so quick to turn away from our colorful minds, saying it's not real. If we ask, Holy Spirit will open our imaginations. Consider this: when God created the world, the first thing He used was His imagination. After imagining it, He spoke the world into being. If our Father used His imagination, then ours must be important. Keep it clean. No porn, no crazy violence or any other junk should get inside your imagination.

> "I pray that the eyes of your heart may be enlightened so that you will know what is the hope of His calling, what are the riches of the glory of His inheritance in the saints." (Ephesians 1:18, NASB 1995)

Worship Jesus:

This is the number one way to see into the spirit realm! Worship Jesus! All power and authority belong to Jesus who now sits at the right hand of God. For Jesus was given authority and dwells in the highest of heavens.

> "Which He brought about in Christ, when He raised Him from the dead and seated Him at His right hand in the heavenly places, far above all rule and authority and power and dominion, and every name that is named, not only in this age but also in the one to come. And He put all things in subjection under His feet and gave Him as head over all things to the church...." (Ephesians 1:20–21, NASB 1995)

> "For this reason, also, God highly exalted Him, and bestowed on Him the name which is above every name, so that at the name of Jesus every knee will bow, of those who are in heaven and on earth and under the earth, and that every tongue will confess that Jesus

Christ is Lord, to the glory of God the Father."
(Philippians 2:9–11, NASB 1995)

Living a lifestyle of adoration toward Jesus is
incredibly important. Do not make the mistake of thinking
that this doesn't matter… angels are attracted to the worship
of Jesus more than anything. Humble yourself before Christ
and adore Him with all your heart and angels will show up
easily! Angels will ride upon your worship! One of my
favorite things to do is to watch angels ride the worship
toward Jesus. It looks like ribbons of colored light, and they
will sit on it with great anticipation. It's funny!

So, You're a Musician:

Good for you! Did you know that angels are attracted to
certain sounds? They love the sound of flutes, violins, drums,
and electric guitar distortions. I remember at my church
watching the electric guitarist play high-pitched sounds and a
whirlwind of angels flew around him in response. As he kept
playing, the angels began to spread around the congregation.
It was so beautiful. Drums will often release angels of warfare
with staffs or swords into the room! They will align and raise
their swords over the congregation!

If you are a singer, sing in the spirit or in your prayer
language. That draws in angels like crazy! My sister is very
good at this. She will sing in the spirit or prophetically, and
angels will float over the stage with long trumpets and bright
golden wings flapping rapidly!

Angels love to worship, even if you worship in your
car. They will sit on top of your car or in the front seat with
you singing! One time I was worshiping the Lord when an
angel flew right in front of the car with his wings outstretched.

It was a good thing I was used to them doing this because I would have swerved my car! The angel in front of my vehicle became translucent, so I could see through him. With his eyes closed, we sang to Jesus together, simple and sweet!

Dance:

Angels love to circle around dancers in worship. I have watched angels mimic a dancer's movement plenty of times and sometimes the dancer will pick up on the angel's movement. Angels, clear like the crystal waters of Heaven, will dance around a person's movement with their wings open and flickering like a gentle flame. If you are a dancer don't stop! Your movement will release them!

Well, folks, those are just some examples or tips for you to engage with the angelic realm. Angels are a normal part of our lives whether we see them or not, but everyone can experience them. Remember, have some humility and take some risks! You haven't lost anything if you're wrong, but don't miss a real encounter because of doubt! Keep on practicing and always, always, always… follow Holy Spirit!

Place your hands over your eyes and heart and pray with me: *Father, in the name of Jesus, I ask that you open my eyes! Holy Spirit, release light into my heart! Holy Spirit, take over my imagination! I surrender it to You! I ask for fire to come upon my heart right now, in Jesus' name! I ask for fire to come upon my eyes, in Jesus' name! Forgive me, Jesus, for dishonoring You with my eyes! I release angels in my life right now, in Jesus' name! Angels, I release you to be active during the day and night, and to be active all around me! I release the revelation of Jesus Christ in my heart! I ask for clarity and understanding in Jesus' name, amen!*

Eden: My Personal Angel

Guardian angels are friends to us, and a great source of encouragement. Your angel is with you from the moment that you're born and stays with you the whole time that you're on Earth. Your guardian angel can look like you, but some angels look more like beasts. For example, some people have winged lions or dragons as angels. Either way, Father, Jesus, and Holy Spirit choose the best angels to assign to you as your guardian angel.

My guardian angel's name is Eden. Eden is the same skin color as I am. He has curly hair like mine, but with silver and gold in it. He has very large wings with a purple and teal color; they're very beautiful. He's taller than me, probably about nine or ten feet tall—a big guy. He wears a robe that is emerald-green, and on his chest occasionally he'll have a picture of a tree, like a full oak tree with gold leaves on it. He has gold embroidery on his sleeve with long streamers that are purple. Eden has very large soft wings that are purple, teal, and white. Recently he was given a new set of wings, so now he has four.

Eden is very kind, excited about everything, loves it when I play video games, watches me closely when I'm preaching, gives me back rubs when needed, and is extremely sociable with my friends. Seriously... he may come to your house if you help with Behold Wonder! Though he is not a ministry angel, he works closely with the ministry angels in my life. Eden's job is to take care of me, not the ministry.

Guardian and Ministry Angels: Eden and Wonder

When I was little, my guardian angel, Eden, used to stand over my crib and use the long purple streamers on his sleeve to play with me. My mom used to tell me that when I was a baby, she would hear me laughing in the night and she would watch me play. She thought I must be playing with angels. Eventually, the Lord took me back in time, and I saw that event. Eden was playing with me using those streamers.

He's a good friend, a very good friend who has walked with me in a lot of areas that I have overcome. That's what's neat about guardian angels. Unlike ministry angels, guardian angels walk with you through the process that you go through; they're a lot closer to you than ministry angels.

Eden and I pray together. We have conversations just like friends do. He knows me very well. He knows when my mind is acting up. When I'm experiencing triggers, Eden will say, "Hey, be careful of that," or "Watch that." He never makes me feel like I am under the situations that trigger me; he always makes me feel like I'm above them. Eden might remind me, "When you're dealing with this, remember that you usually think this way, so guard yourself." He's always encouraging me to gird and fortify my mind in the word of God.

Eden and I worship God together a lot. He's always around when I worship God; in fact, sometimes Eden invites other angel friends over to worship with us. I told him that he could invite them to join us.

If my encounters with the Lord are going to be difficult ones, Eden will be present to watch me and make sure I get back to my body safely. He'll also call for angelic assistance if he knows that he needs help with certain assignments. Eden will call stronger angels to assist him and help take care of things.

There was one point where I battled anxiety a lot. I would wake up in the middle of the night, sometimes with demons trying to torment me. But there would also be times when I would wake up and Eden would be wrestling a demon, holding him down, pinning him. He would always smile and say, "I've taken care of it. Go back to sleep, it's okay," and I would fall right back to sleep. I felt so much peace from Eden's presence.

Eden's a hand-to-hand combat guy so he doesn't use weapons much, but mostly uses his hands and fists to wrestle with demons. He uses his hands to grapple with them. When he really needs to up his game to defend, he'll turn into a giant white bear with gold claws and gold on the tips of his fur. When Eden becomes a bear, he's huge! He is already ten feet tall, so you can imagine how big the bear is! When Eden is a bear, he will crush demons with his mouth if he needs to step up and take care of things.

Now the ministry angel assigned to me, Wonder, is very different. He has giant wings as well, but his wings are purple and white. The first time I met Wonder was in the home of my pastors, Van and Laurie Cochrane. I was in their basement attending a house group meeting for young adults, and we were doing ministry time. I was laying on the floor and went into the spirit world. I saw a beautiful angel come down and tell me his name was "Wonder". That was the first time that I met Wonder. He told me that he'll be with me when I minister and will be responsible for releasing the presence of the Lord and opening heaven.

Wonder has very long white hair that has diamonds in it, so it sparkles when the light shines on it. His hair is so long that it looks like it is going to touch the floor, but it never does; instead, it hovers above the floor. Sometimes his hair will be down and long, and sometimes he likes to wear it in a low bun.

Wonder is smaller than Eden, maybe 7 or 8 feet tall. People will sometimes see him as a halo around me, or a figure in white above me and walking behind me, or as a light, or as wings behind me while I'm ministering or in meetings talking.

Wonder wears a robe of purple and gold with a gold tie or belt around his waist. His robe doesn't have any sleeves; it's like a muscle shirt.

Eden is my guardian angel and helps with growth, discipline, and personal development. He travels with me for protection and to keep watch.

Wonder is the angel that's with me while I'm teaching and ministering. He's there with me keeping me filled up and giving me ideas... he will assign and direct angels under him who work with Behold Wonder and our Prophetic School to do certain things. He's the one who stays closest to me when I'm talking.

More about Eden

When I was little, I always felt that an extra presence or an extra friend was with me in some way.

My parents used to say when I was still sleeping in the crib in their room, that I would be awake in the middle of the night, lying on my back, laughing and kicking and looking up at the ceiling. My parents believed that I was talking to angels.

I remember one day when I was about 17 years old, Eden appeared to me. We talked about the ministry of guardian angels and what they do and how they feel. That conversation was just as if I was interviewing him. Eden took me back in time and showed me a vision of myself lying in the crib, kicking and laughing, and having a good time. I saw Eden looking over my crib. Eden had these beautiful streamers on his wrist, and he was playing with me, making the streamers go across my face. As a baby, I was just kicking and laughing and screaming and enjoying it. Then I realized that what my parent's thought was so true; Eden was playing with me even then!

Eden told me that he couldn't wait for me to come out of my mom's womb and see the earth for the first time. Eden enjoyed being around my mom and watching and looking after me while I was in her womb.

One thing I want to say about guardian angels: they are very powerful, wonderful friends. You may not know that your guardian angel really feels for you. Your guardian angel understands you and was created to do so. Your guardian angel is there to fight for you and stick up for you when evil comes your way and tries to take you out. Your guardian angel is healing you. Many times, your angel has saved your life!

One of the most powerful things about the ministry of guardian angels that I've noticed by having Eden in my life and watching guardian angels around others is that not only do guardian angels protect you physically, but they also protect you emotionally. They really do care for you, and they provide emotional support to you when you feel lonely, depressed, or sad.

Angels are not like robots that just hang around you and look stoic! When you're sad, they feel sadness. When you are angry, they can feel the anger. Angels do what they can to bring you into God's reality.

Your guardian angel is very personal to you and is excited about the things you're excited about. I remember playing the video game *Street Fighter* when I was a kid. I would get frustrated trying to defeat the Boss and would hear Eden behind me cry out, "Oh man!" when I would lose the battle. I would turn around and look at Eden behind me, and he would have this expression on his face like, "Oh yeah, you can see me!"

One time Eden said, "Try doing this move," and he grabbed the controller, and performed a move that I had not yet learned with that character. "When you try this move, get low down on the ground and hit this button." That's how I finally beat the Boss in *Street Fighter*. It was so much fun! It was cool because even in the small things, like beating a character in a game, Eden the angel was there helping me.

All guardian angels are awesome! The Lord really gave Eden to me as a gift, as He gave your guardian angel to you. Father always gives His best to us![2]

I've learned from Eden that whenever you see little flashes or sparkles like little glimmers around you at random times, that's angelic activity. Eden said, "That's when I am surrounding you with my wings. I would love for you to notice." I thought to myself, Eden wants me to notice when he is saying hello or saying that he's with me. I looked at Eden when he said that to me, and I realized he doesn't want any glory or worship. He just wants to be my friend, and he wants to be appreciated. Appreciating angels is not the same as worshiping them, it's just being friendly. Ever since I was little, I would say "Hello," to Eden or tell him "Thank you," or how much I appreciated him. Do you know what happened? It didn't distract my attention from God, but, in fact, it heightened my awareness of my love for Father, Son, and Holy Spirit. Whenever you really appreciate a gift, you will be drawn to the Creator.

So, I want to tell you that it's okay to appreciate your angels because when you do that it draws you to the Creator God. It shows you just how awesome our Creator is and how beautiful He is, and how much of a personal lovely Father He is. He loves you, and He always wants to give to you His best gifts. One of the best gifts He can give you is a guardian angel to look after you, care for you, and give you emotional and physical support. Your guardian angel is someone who sees you, is a friend to you, and who will be with you for your entire journey on Earth. I thank God so much for creating Eden. I thank the Lord so much for loving me and giving me a friend as I was growing up.

I see angels not as robotic spirit beings, but as companions with unique personalities. They give up their lives to serve the Lord and to look after you. Yes, angels have lives! They are choosing to serve the Lord and serve you.

A Conversation with Eden

Eden looked at me with slight sadness, "Our goal is to bring you closer to your Father, whom we love too." Eden lowered his head, looking at the crystal sea flowing under our feet, "It's always been about knowing God." I reached for his hand and held it. He was a little startled by my touch, but smiled kindly, looking into my eyes.

I ensured Eden looked at me, "Thank you for your help. I am sorry we do not appreciate you well. We believe so many lies that we forget that your mission is not easy. I apologize for the humans who forget to show their appreciation. Some of them just don't know, Eden."

Eden lightly squeezed my hand with a smile, tilting his head to the left. He bashfully wiped away his tears quickly. He said with a sigh, "We love God so much; even if we do not always understand His ways, we choose to love Him. We won't leave Him either. Just like you, Micah. We won't leave you because you are His greatest love. And..." the angel said, putting his hand on my shoulder, "We love you too." This time a tear fell on his cheek.

I embraced him abruptly, saying, "Thank you. Thank you all so much for helping us."

As Eden and I embraced, I could feel his stomach bouncing from laughter and his tears of gratitude on my cheek. "You are welcome," he said as he pressed his cheek against mine in our embrace.

Remember your guardian angels today. When was the last time you thanked your guardian angel for their assistance? No, we do not worship angels; we worship God only. However, we do not want to forget our help and friends who stand with us along the way, right? Even if you cannot see your angels right now, turn to your left or right and thank them. They will appreciate your kindness, which is a great way to start interacting with them.

Angels That Encourage Us

Minister of Rest:

As I waited for the Lord, an angel appeared next to me with a bowl of crystal-clear water that had purple flowers in it. I felt such peace that I got incredibly sleepy. I tried to keep my eyes open–the angel giggled at my attempt to stay awake.

This lovely blue angel had long black hair that shimmered in the light coming from his chest. He did not appear to have wings, but I could feel a refreshing breeze coming from him.

My new friend asked, "Why do you fight against resting?"

I yawned, "I don't know. Things don't seem to get done."

The angel nodded his head with understanding, then encouraged me, "Rest is the most important key to wanting to be effective in the Kingdom. So many people want to 'do' things for Him but will not rest. Not resting will cause you to be a nesting ground for the enemy. To rule with power, you must rest. Rule with rest... with resting you rule." The angel laughed at his wordplay. I, on the other hand, was so peaceful that the angel's voice was becoming barely audible.

As I lay there, the angel poured the bowl of water on my head, and he blessed me saying, "Son of light and son of His love, it is time to rule with resting! Have peace now...."

I fell asleep.

The Angel of Purity:

"Hi," my new friend greeted me.

"Hello, good morning," I said back to him.

Angels are delightful to have around.

During my 6 a.m. routine, angels come and go. We worship and pray together and sometimes they like to read with me! But this new friend, dressed in a brilliant white robe and large wings of light, wanted to tell me something.

He held my hands and said, "You are already pure, you just have bad habits. To get rid of those habits, replace them with something new and beautiful. You know... it takes practice to walk out what is yours. Purity is already given to you; your Father gives grace because He knows habits can be challenging." He paused for a moment—then as if he had a great idea, he said, "To help you practice walking in purity, live in a place of worship and praise, which is the entryway to His presence. There are many other ways you can practice walking in purity, which is another way of saying, 'walking in His presence'. Get creative and replace those bad habits... it's possible to get rid of them all. You just have to put in the work, and they will go!"

He stood up and smiled, but then remembered something else, "There is something else I want to say too. Purity is strengthened in a place of intimacy with Him, which brings a greater sense of power. When you walk in purity you will see the power of God manifest in your life, so it is important that you live in what has already been given to you."

My angel friend jumbled my hair and then disappeared, but later reappeared again, "I am going to help you out too! My name is Purity. Ok, I love you. Bye-bye!"

He vanished.

Thank you, Jesus! We love you!

The Angels Beauty and Holiness:

As I sat with God, I felt a gentle breeze rush by me. I knew angels had entered the room, so I looked to see who my new visitors were.

Two beautiful angels with kind eyes stood in front of me. Their innocent hearts showed through their eyes. As I studied them more, I realized they were identical twins. Everything about them was remarkably similar. The only difference was their robes.

"It is so good to meet you," one said as he reached for my hand.

"We have heard so much about you." The other added, "Now we have come to be a part of your walk on the Earth." He was delighted to be a part of my life.

"Hi! My name is Micah. What are your names?" I shook both of their hands. It is nice to be polite to angels! Even though they are His servants, they still are "people" and have hearts like everyone else. Being polite and courteous is good.

The first one answered by placing his hand on his chest, "I am Beauty, and this is my brother, Holiness."

They both stood together and bowed at the waist, "At your service."

Beauty held true to his name. He was beautiful! He wore a long robe that was light blue and that flashed with light. The fabric design resembled roses opening to the sunlight. He had a crown of bright blue roses on top of his curly blond hair. I could tell that this angel's skin tone was like a shiny cluster of pearls. Beauty had deep blue eyes that sparkled with curiosity and joy. He looked at me with wonder and amazement.

His twin brother, Holiness, had a skin tone that was also like shining pearls, only he had a crown of white roses on top of his curly blond hair. He had a white robe with a silver mantle on his shoulders. Flashes of light and a cloud of glory were inside the angel's gown. I could tell Holiness loved his brother very much because he kept looking back at him.

Both angels were proud to be with me and they smiled, rocking back and forth on their heels.

I enjoyed them. I asked, "What has Father sent you to tell me?" and sat down to listen.

They spoke together, "Worship the Lord in beauty; worship the Lord in holiness. It is sweet to the Lord! We have come to help you walk in what you are created to be."

Then the angels looked at each other as if they had planned the next trick in a show. They stepped into each other–forming one being. I gasped, as they became one beautiful angel of glory.

Again, I gasped as this angel's light created a rainbow in my room. I could smell the sweet fragrance of God's presence at that moment. The angel said, "Yes, holiness is beauty from within that changes the world on the outside of you. It all begins from within your heart. If you wish to walk in greatness, then you need to love the beauty of holiness."

They disappeared.

Angels are incredible servants of God who are committed to seeing you live in the fullness of Christ manifested through you. They walk among us every day, waiting for moments to encourage us or simply to have fun with us! If your heart is open and you believe, you will see them walking right next to you as friends. *Father, thank you so much for giving your children help to encourage us throughout our journey. Thank you, Father, for the angels.*

Samuel and the Cold Prophet

I was going through a somewhat difficult season at the beginning of 2012. I felt extremely alone. I had wonderful friends and family reach out to me, but my heart was cold. I was confused, hurt, and angry at God but I couldn't hate Him, I just wanted to know if He understood the hardship through which I was walking. Please read the encounter below. Some people think that just because I see into Heaven and have face-to-face encounters, I do not struggle. May you remember that the Prophets/Seers need Jesus very much! We will always need Him! May this encourage you!

I was alone one cold evening, pondering about my life and all that is to happen and has happened. The snow drifted over my shoes while I sat alone on a swing set. I had been going through some very hard warfare the previous few months and felt my strength fleeing from me. I whispered to God as I waited for Him to speak. I didn't quite have tears anymore; I had used them all up. I just wanted to have the strength to make it through one more day.

I waited... no answer. I waited longer... I couldn't hear God's voice.

I sighed and felt invisible. "Jesus, I need your help. I just don't feel like I can do this anymore. It's so hard right now. I am trying my best to remain faithful to you; I don't know why I feel so alone."

That was my last attempt to wait for Him; I didn't know if He would come. I thought I would try again tomorrow. Suddenly, a peculiar man approached me.

He was dressed in a white t-shirt and had regular blue jeans on; nothing stood out about him. His green eyes smiled, "May I sit here?" He tucked his silver hair behind his ear to prepare for my answer.

I shrugged my shoulders, "Sure. My name is Micah."

The man smiled, "I am Samuel. I know who you are, and I know you very well. I watch you swing here often." He cleared his throat and paused for a moment to sit down. He sat up straight; crossed his left leg and scratched his nose. He took a deep breath and stared right at me.

I broke the silence, "It's cold out here." I didn't want my new friend, who I assumed was an angel, to think I was not in the mood to talk. "Aren't you cold?"

He looked at His arms, "Nope, I am not cold. I don't get cold, but the world is cold, is it not?" He looked at me, "The world is always cold, but Jesus is the warm light of the sun. That sunlight is in you, my friend." He said as he rubbed my shoulders trying to warm me.

I smirked.

Samuel just kept looking at me and I looked away. I could feel compassion coming from him; he genuinely cared for me, but I just couldn't talk to him.

Samuel asked, "Micah, what is it that you want the Lord to do for you?"

I burst out in anger, "I don't want to feel alone anymore. I am tired of feeling like I don't fit in." I hit the angel's leg, "I see you and hear you, but I don't feel like I am on the right planet. I feel so weak and forgotten by Jesus."

The angel placed his arm around me and caught my tears. In a gentle tone he said, "Micah, need I remind you, you asked for a heart that would be entirely His. You asked for His world and that His fire would be your bread, and that His blood would be your water to drink. You are angry with Him for the gift He has given you. You cannot be of this world and be living in His." The angel lifted my sorrowful head and spoke to me, "You are not alone, Micah. You have family and friends whom God has created to see you. When you feel the cold world around you, go and sit in the sunlight of God who lives in those He has placed in your life. God is light."

"But sir, I don't feel the warmth." I placed my hands in his, "My hands are cold."

The angel began to warm them, "You believe they do not know that you feel or have needs. Micah, Jesus is everything you need, and in placing your hands in His, your needs will be met. That doesn't mean you will not need a community; it means that in seeking Him you will find that community because Jesus is always with His people."

The angel placed my hands on my heart and disappeared; then I heard Jesus say, "Micah, I heard you. Now get up and walk forward!"

I stood up as the setting sun's rays touched my face. I felt His love once again and I knew I could make it through this season. I wanted to thank the angel for his encouragement, but he did not return.

Perhaps I won't see him anymore… I do not know.

Jesus, I love you!

Prophecy Without Love

I came home from work, walked into my apartment, and noticed some angels were there, which isn't anything new. They were talking to each other and when they noticed I had come into the room, they grabbed some pots and pans and metal spoons, and they started banging on the pans and following me around making noise.

At first, I thought it was funny, but it got very obnoxious and loud, and I got annoyed with them. I turned to them and said, "What are you doing?"

They said, "You are annoying without love," and turned around and walked out of the room. Then Holy Spirit said, "If you don't have love, you are an annoying cymbal."[3] I learned that day that more than anything, I wanted to be filled with love. More than having answers to all the mysteries, I want to know love, be love, and have love move outside of me and through me.

Michael: The Day the Stars Fell

In this visitation, I met Michael and heard his perspective on the fall of Lucifer. Angels are created beings who serve us, but they also need the presence and power of God as we do. They are not sons, scripture is clear on that, but they are ministering spirits sent to us! Please read the narrative of this angelic visitation.

I remember one moment, I was listening to Michael speak of the Falling Stars, an event in which Lucifer and all those who sided with him fell from Heaven. The angel with me made sure I listened to Michael because this was a very tender moment. He said that the day Lucifer fell from Heaven the angelic order changed. The angels have a sense of family among them, and it was death and destruction that day as those whom they loved fell into darkness. Michael, the angelic prince, was looking over a terrace of beautiful waterfalls into the dimension below him. I had never seen this side of him previously. Michael's heart was carried away in song as his giant, fiery, bronze wings lifted.

This mighty angel of God had huge wings of burning bronze with sparks of fire at the tip of every feather. He had a golden sash around his chest that said his name. He had long black hair that shimmered with the fire of God. He was huge—at least 15 ft tall with two enormous swords on his side—and he was incredibly muscular! It looked as though he had gold in his skin, which blazed with the glorious presence of God that's inside him.

As I approached Michael he spoke, "There was silence. Heaven was shaken. I saw them fall like comets from the sky. Their terrible screams of death cursed them. Lucifer was thrown away by my own hand. The shaking of fear tangled his throat, but I was focused... focused on God. I needed Him that day. We all did." Michael turned to me with his arms crossed. His wings moved up and down... powerfully... they flicked fire into the atmosphere. Michael was so powerful, but I could see vulnerability in his eyes. He needed the Creator just like we do. Michael needed Jesus just like we do. I began to understand this angel more as I looked into his eyes. He is strong, mighty and unwavering in righteousness, but he is just an angel, given authority by God to do His work. Yes, they are much stronger than we are, but they are dependent upon the light of God. Michael took a deep breath and leaned forward so I could see his eyes much more clearly. His voice was soft now, "I need Jesus too, Micah. I'm not trodden down by sin or darkness, but I cannot exist without the light. The reason I fight for Israel, for you, is because Jesus burns within me. His fire gives me strength to overcome the powers of darkness. It is by His wisdom that I can lead countless angels into battle. We are created by His infinite power. Out of the gems of the sea we are born. By the winds of fire are we conceived."

I could see the story of the falling angels in his eyes. He became emotional but dismissed it by turning away quickly. "You have seen my heart. You saw the place of need for Him, Micah. It is time to go home now."

The angel who was with me stepped in between us, saying nothing, but obeyed Michael's orders. He indicated with a smile that I should walk away. I turned around to walk back toward the portal, but I could still hear Michael singing his song to God over the noise of the waterfalls. The angel with me said, "This is where it happened, where the stars fell into the darkness. He comes here every now and again to sing and remember God's goodness."

Angels are created too, and Father takes care of them just like you and me. If He looks after the gentle spirit of angels, how much more are those born from His heart? You are greatly loved, friends!

The Angel Gabriel

This is about the first encounter I had with Gabriel. It was such a blessing to be encouraged by one of God's messengers! I did my best to write this so that through His angel you would all receive encouragement from God to walk in your destiny as sons of God. Enjoy!

One day while considering the skies of Heaven, among the stars appeared one star shining in brilliant blue. Its glow was like a flowing fountain of light. I was amazed at its beauty among the stars of Heaven. In a moment, the stars began to unfold into one of the most beautiful angels I had ever seen. He was tall and dressed in a blazing blue robe. It looked like this angel was created with blue lightning, which showed from beneath his robe. Beautiful! His face was almost bronze, and he had white hair. At the tip of each strand of hair were colors that gave him a soft glow! A bright cloud covered his feet. His large sparkling wings were silver light! The other stars in the sky made way for this mighty angel, then circled around him. There must have been angels hidden in the twilight who brightened the sky! The great angel introduced himself properly with a gentle nod of the head, "I am Gabriel. One of the Four Great Stars of Heaven."

What beautiful light this angel carried inside his being! The angel said, "I know who you are, Micah Turnbo. Present yourself with confidence to me."

I stood up straight saying, "My name is Micah Turnbo." Then Gabriel extended his hand to welcome me. Gabriel raised his trumpet and blew it toward the stars in Heaven. In doing so, a loud sound pierced through me! The clouds rushed away as the framework of the sky shook! I could see the Earth in front of me as Gabriel investigated it. His bright silver wings moved back and forth in response to the presence of God among us!

Then the angel said, "This is the time! Yes, the greatest time that has ever been upon the Earth, where angels and men will release the destiny of God. Every dimension, dominion, and reality has been longing for the day when men will accept their identity as sons of God. For by them the order will be restored to the heavens, and the throne of the Son of God will be set upon the earth. Every name will call Him Jesus Christ, King of Kings and Lord of Lords Prepare for the cleansing to come by fire, oh sons of God. Prepare for the darkness that comes to eat away the destiny given to you. Remain faithful! Remain strong in the Lord."

Gabriel's wings extended about 20 feet and he said, "I am a messenger and those who lift their eyes to the heavens shall hear the angels declare their longing for the completion of the fullness of time and the beginning of eternity!" He looked at me and said, "To you Micah, it has been given before the foundations of the world, to sit with Christ–to rule and reign with Him. Beware of distractions! Fear is a distraction! Shame, the promise of worldly riches, and unforgiveness are distractions in the world. Do not give in to them. The promise of man's fame is but dust of the earth." Gabriel's voice became loud like thunder, "To God be the glory! To God be the riches! In His hand are pleasures forevermore!"

Then the angel became emotional, and I saw his vulnerability, "We love you, Micah. We love His children and have given ourselves to serve Him, which means helping you achieve the highest call given to you! By the Holy Spirit's power upon us, we are given much to aid you... do not take the distractions of man's hand. Do not eat of the worldly pleasures." He flew close to me, and the cloud of glory covered me! He placed his big hand on my shoulder and said, "You and I... we are partners by the power of Holy Spirit! By the love and grace of God, we will spread the name of Jesus Christ across the Earth!"

Gabriel turned around to blow his trumpet to the remaining stars in the sky which now had become blue angels like he was! He faced me once again, "I have been given a company of angels to send with those who will press into their calling!" Suddenly, lightning flashed in front of my eyes, and Gabriel, with his company of angels, was gone. The sky had returned to normal!

"The time is now," the voice of Holy Spirit said in my heart. "The angels of God are ready! They are ready to carry the gospel of Jesus Christ. Like you, they shine in the darkness to bring hope!"

[1] "For He will command His angels concerning you to guard you in all your ways." (Psalm 91:11, ESV)

[2] "Every gift God freely gives us is good and perfect, streaming down from the Father of lights, who shines from the heavens with no hidden shadow or darkness and is never subject to change." (James 1:17, TPT)

[3] "If I speak in the tongues of men and of angels, but have not love, I am a noisy gong or a clanging cymbal." (1 Corinthians 13:1, ESV)

Chapter 10

Fighting the Dark Side

Chapter Outline:

- Wisdom Tips for Fighting Demons

- The Webspinner

- The Power of Our Voice

- The Tomb of the Watchers

- Why Satan Attacks Us

Wisdom Tips for Fighting Demons

What should I do when I see demons? Here is what I have learned from experience.

1. Many demons are stupid. Yes, I said stupid. However, their stupidity does not mean they cannot communicate with you and spin lies to you. I never talk to demons unless I am commanded to do so by the Lord in a strategic way.

2. Seeking out demons is also stupid. They will reveal themselves on their own if you are a threat to them. Seeking them out is asking for trouble even if you love deliverance. If the power that is in you is real, you do not need to be a demon

hunter. Most of the time your presence is enough to drive them away without you even commanding them to leave.

3. If you see a demon oppressing someone, telling the person immediately is stupid. Don't do that. Go to Holy Spirit and ask Him what to do next. When I see demons on someone, I rarely tell them; I speak the exact opposite of what the demon is trying to do. When I speak the word of the Lord over someone my words are like fire. At times, just the word of the Lord is enough to prevent the demonic spirit from affecting a person.

4. There are times to cast a demon out as Jesus did in Matthew 8:16¹ and times you must leave it. Trust me, not every deliverance is supposed to be done by you. Wisdom is knowing when and when not to cast out demons.

5. You don't need to shout. Demons can hear you just fine. I watched a demon saying to a person who kept shouting, mostly out of insecurity, "I am not deaf, dummy. Geez!" Authority is not determined by how much you raise your voice. If it's real, then Heaven moves at the sound of your whisper.

6. When casting out a demon with a team, pick a leader to perform the deliverance. Demons are not intelligent and sometimes they get confused. Not all of you need to speak. Let one perform the deliverance and the others support with prayer and prophetic insight. If you are the support during a deliverance prayer your role is to support the leader.

7. If you see or sense a demon in your house, kick it out. You don't have to freak out. Demons are like flies! Swat them and get them out of your house. Sometimes flies get into your house. Squash 'em in Jesus' name. I say phrases like, "In

the name of Jesus Christ, get out of my house now," or "Get out of here!" I just say what comes to me by Holy Spirit. I have authority in Jesus' name, and they know that.

The Webspinner

It is not often that I share my encounters with demons, but I wish to share this encounter, or rather, the Lord has asked me to share it. Please read the short story below with a heart to understand so that you may know the kingdom of darkness.

Spiders began to fall from my ceiling as if their legs reached out for me. Their webs were not typical; they glowed green like they were poisonous. I was startled by this, so I tried to swat the spiders away.

The atmosphere changed. I had entered a very unclean realm. Sharp rocks with all kinds of terrifying bugs crawling on them surrounded me. The sky was blood red with floating spider eyes. The bugs turned into demonic beings that cried out in wicked screams toward me. They appeared as gangly and deformed beasts, like rotting flesh. Their clawed hands oozed some kind of bile that smelled terrible.

"Lord!" I cried out, "Get me out of here, please! Help me!" Coming from the distance, a dark being approached me. He was in a black royal robe with emerald jewels embedded in the fabric. He was wearing a crown of worms around his head. His pointed ears were pierced with ornaments. There was a ring of thorns around his middle finger that nested a yellow diamond. He was escorted by two walking demons of rotting flesh. These two flesh demons were chained together by the demonic prince who had come to meet with me.

The surrounding demons moaned as the demonic prince came closer. He inspected my form. I felt sick to my stomach when he smiled as if I was pleasurable to him. He was not Satan, but part of Satan's government. You can say, this "prince" once served God but now is in darkness. This demonic prince introduced himself with a bow from the waist.

"I am The Webspinner, and I wish to make a deal with you. Let us come to an agreement. You have caused many problems in my domain, Micah. If you serve me, The Webspinner, you may have some of my lands and I will take your voice." He stepped closer, "I am no warrior. I work in the office. These worms that you call demons serve me, much like how the angels serve you. You may keep them… I just want your voice. It is good for us to make a deal." He stepped even closer and whispered, "Come, Satan doesn't have to know. Come join my domain. If I had the power, I would sit on his throne. I want to take his throne to be my own, but I need power. The sons of… the…." He could not finish saying the words "the sons of God" because even that title carried too much anointing.

I turned my eyes away, "Father help me!" I would not look at him any longer.

"Webspinner!" Another sinister voice called from among the webs of this fallen domain. Lucifer had descended from above with his feet dripping in some kind of bile. His dirty feet made me nauseous. "I was passing by when I heard you voicing schemes against me… you are like a spider toying with its prey before you devour it."

The Webspinner stepped back from me, "Keep your mouth shut."

He bowed to Satan, "My lord, you have come…." The Webspinner raised his hands, using his powers to light up the area, and revealing the entire land covered in spider webs and filthy creatures.

"This one is mine…." He threatened Satan while changing into a massive spider….

Spider legs emerged out of the stomach of The Webspinner. Even the demons who were under his leadership screeched with great contempt at The Webspinner's true form—a spider of great poisons from the demonic realm. His domain shook at the might of such a terrible monstrosity.

Satan smirked, "You dare resist me. I am the one who made your ring. I showed you how to attain your crown of worms. You spew witchcraft because of me and now you battle against the rightful king?"

The Webspinner's voice was now cruel, "You are not welcome in my domain! Curse you! You hoard your gifts like a dragon who sleeps in its stolen gold. You know nothing of these creatures who claim to have authority over you." The Webspinner was talking about me, "He is mine. I will sit on your throne!"

Satan roared as his eyes changed to red like a violent beast. Coming from his back was a pair of dragon wings in frightening black smoke. Satan threatened The Webspinner, "You, I will tear you apart starting with your legs. I will rip you apart! Give me that man of God."

Satan, with great fury, pulled a sword from his chest and assaulted the spider. His sword had a great eye near the handle that appeared to be bleeding all over his hands. It was once a beautiful sword, but now it resembled the lust for blood in his heart. Satan thrived on chaos and violence.

The Webspinner was a manipulator of terrible magic. I am unsure if he was more powerful in his own domain, but he used stone relics that hovered around his form as a source for enchanting. His eight eyes glowed the green of witchcraft. Perhaps this is where such powers are acquired—from the demon they serve—The Webspinner.

He could control the webs that covered the area and use them like ghoulish clawed hands to crush his victims; by using his telepathic abilities, The Webspinner summoned countless other spiders and demonic creatures to fight for him.

Satan cut the smaller demons down in mad laughter. Yes, he was crazy... murder made him crazy! I could see how much these beings had fallen from the grace and beauty God had once given them.

They were fighting over me, over my voice. The two princes wanted my authority. I did not know what else to do but stand still. I didn't want to move. I will admit I was afraid.

I called out to the Lord for help again and again. As I covered my head I screamed, "Help me!"

Suddenly, the atmosphere changed, and I heard thunder approaching. A loud voice echoed, "Enough!" A great and powerful bolt of lightning crashed in between The Webspinner's army and Satan, separating them. It was a stream of liquid light from above them, so blinding to the demons that they moaned in terrible pain. Stepping out of the light was a mighty angel.

Michael had stepped out of the light wearing golden armor, with fiery glory coming from his eyes. He used his bronze wings of light to push back The Webspinner and Satan. Like children, the two demons threw tantrums.

Michael said with authority, "Back up now!"

Satan relinquished his attacks and turned to leave. He mocked The Webspinner's failed attempts to overrule the lord of darkness' throne. Satan's wings lowered as he walked away, "Cross me again, Webspinner, and I will burn your realm to the ground." Satan entered a portal of darkness to his fallen castle and then vanished.

The Webspinner was not pleased with Michael's presence. He cursed Michael again and again. His language was horrible. I will not write what he said to the angel during his moment of defeat.

I felt the Lord's peace come into my spirit as Michael looked towards me with a slight smile as if to say, *you will be alright*. I dropped to my knees. I was tired.

The Webspinner said, "You! I hate you! Get out of my way!" He tried to muster strength against Michael's power, but it was not enough. The angelic prince stabbed him, as quick as light. I could hear the demonic prince's bones breaking.

The Webspinner squealed in excruciating pain as his guts fell out of him. His realm trembled in distress too. They were connected. The Webspinner stumbled back, "No! No! Look what you've done…." He vanished.

Michael turned to me once more as this demonic realm tumbled apart. He dashed toward me, picking me up, "You will be alright, Micah. The Lord is always with you. We must leave quickly."

We launched into the sky to escape the domain of The Webspinner. As Michael and I ascended the angel dodged falling stones swiftly, "We are almost there. Make sure you breathe." I held onto him as tightly as I could.

In one last push against the falling stones, Michael and I reached clear skies above the demonic domain and entered Heaven.

The reason I share this encounter is so that you understand the power of your voice in the spirit realm. The angels understand its value and seek to protect it. The demons and fallen spirits understand it and seek to control you; to use you. May we surrender our hearts to God.

The Power of Our Voice

I am going to be focusing on demons from a different approach. We all fight against shadows in the light, or the monster under our beds. The problem is we never talk about them because we fear them. My goal in sharing this is for you to know how powerful your voice is.

Demons... they are lousy! They are lazy, and if they can get you to do their work for them, they will. They will take a catnap right in your home without you even noticing; we so quickly empower them to stay. It turns out that our voice can do two things: empower demons or disempower demons. Yes, you can strengthen a demon's activity around you. Now, of course, engaging in outright sin welcomes demons and drains us, but most of the time they suck us dry because of the negative things we say about ourselves. In my case, that was happening!

There was a time a demon was following me around day and night. He was a black beast with red eyes! Just looking at his teeth sucked the life out of me. I knew I had angels around; I would see them! Two angels in front and two in back. They looked at me intently as if to say, "What are you going to do?" I would turn around and rebuke the demon, and it would disappear, but return later.

Sometimes this nasty critter would prowl in my room! I would wake up to the demon hitting me and incredible fear would enter the room! I would look up, and there would be a warrior angel above me watching me, but he had the same look on his face, "What are you going to do?" I noticed the angel did not have a weapon! That was alarming!

For a few weeks, this demon would come and go until finally, I had had enough! I felt horrible! How am I hosting a demon? Father, help me! Then out of nowhere, I began to say out loud how dumb I felt and how stupid I was acting. I started to say horrible things about myself. Wow! As these words just slipped out of my mouth the demon began to growl! He grew more hideous too. As I spoke those things about myself, I watched the demon consume the negative energy I was spewing! I immediately stopped talking.

When the demon realized he was not getting any more food from me, he began to roar like a hungry predator. He stood up on his hind legs and showed his claws.

I must admit I was scared; terror gripped my heart. As the demon roared, I heard a gentle voice inside me say, "Use your voice again, but this time say the exact opposite of what you said before now."

Of course, that was Holy Spirit giving me instruction, so I obeyed Him. I started to speak positive things and I was amazed at what happened! The demon began to shrink!

He started to scream loud curses at me as power drained from him. The nasty beast rolled on the floor in pain! What was I saying, you ask? Well, I was just saying the kind of things Jesus would say about me! Then it turned into praise of how God is faithful to me. That's right, I started to watch as God's power flowed from my mouth by simply saying good and true things about myself which turned into how great He is. Light filled the room as I worshiped God. The demon was set on fire by the Lord's presence. Its flesh was melting off its bony structure.

Suddenly an angel reappeared with a long sword of light! I hadn't noticed his sword before now.

I asked the angel, "Where was your weapon before?"

The angel looked at me, "I didn't have one yet. Your praise and positivity gave me a weapon to use against Him! Sometimes we wait to get our gear from you! When you start to worship and praise it gives us powerful weapons against the enemy."

After the angel said this, he stabbed the demon, and its guts went everywhere. The beast moaned as its body slid down the blade of light wielded by the angel. Praise God!

The angel looked at me, "Good job!" He left.

I was stunned by what I just learned about spiritual warfare and how demons are not as powerful as we think. They feed off our negative energy through the things we say about ourselves, or even believe about ourselves! We have got to think better than they do! We have got to speak over our spirit what God says about us! There will be no victory when we talk with negativity; it only increases their power over us.

If you are going through spiritual warfare, I encourage you to get into God's presence and worship Him. Release angels in your room and praise God as loud as you can! Find a quiet place and sing. Speak good, healthy things into the air and over your spirit. Speak promises God has spoken to you out loud. Demons will lose their strength!

Use your voice!

Your voice can bring life or bring death![2] It can strengthen angels or strengthen demons.

The Tomb of the Watchers

Watchers are a type of angel mentioned in Daniel 4, who come with authority to speak God's message. Some rebelled as in Jude 6, wanting their own power, and are awaiting judgment deep in the earth.

Some have said that deep in the earth, within the spirit world, there are 300 tombs. I've had experiences that seem to validate that. Fallen once-wise spiritual beings who gave in to their lust for power, the Watchers wait in their tombs for judgment. Now they are decaying, rotting in darkness, never to see the light again until the day of their judgment.[3] They will stand once more before their former King and beg for forgiveness, but they will not receive it. They will be thrown into the fire of eternal judgment; a death that is worse than they can imagine.

As I watched them, chained forever in their tombs, I could see that their forms had been burrowed through by countless worms like sacks of abominations. Chains of burning fire bound their bodies forever and their moans filled the deep caverns of the underground caves.

At the gate of their tombs, a mighty angel holding a spear of golden light paced back and forth on a horse of fire to keep watch over their prison so that no demon may break them free. Not even Satan can pass.

Carved in the stone gate like claws reaching out to grab you, the name of such a dark place is written in an angelic tongue. In the tongue of humans, it says 'Oblivion,' a name fitting for the 300 Watchers bound to their death, lying in their tombs.

Yes, this is the history of the Earth. Deep below, the Watchers are buried. Oh, that you would hear the moans of their banished souls, that you would never forget how much the King of Kings paid for your salvation. Death does not have to be your future.

Remember the Watchers.

Why Satan Attacks Us

There are times I feel sadness, bordering on pity, for Satan, this beautiful creation of God that is now fallen.

I may surprise you when I say this, but I do. I have seen Satan's past, his beauty, goodness, and kindness from before he fell. I have also seen his complete darkness.

People often ask me what he looks like, and I always say he looks very lonely, depressed, and rejected. Evil spills from him; yes, it's true. However, he feels sadness more than anything in his heart, and it is a fate of his own doing.

When I see him act out violence, it comes from a place of a broken soul—someone who doesn't feel loved at all. When I see him spill human blood it comes from a deep place of hating himself. He hates himself so he hates everyone else.

His depression keeps him locked away in his castle… he drowns his pain with the finest wines he can make to forget his past when he had everything. His rooms are still full of treasure, pleasure, and gifts, but dust covers them like snow.

He is alone, trapped in his fate forever. He looks through the windows of grief, never to experience joy, happiness, freedom, or love again. His shame is like snow falling upon his cold heart.[4]

Why am I sharing this? Because when you see Satan correctly, you understand why he attacks us with those things. His greatest fear, greatest loss, is that he is not loved, and so he attacks you with his truth which is the lie humans battle every day. It is never a question of how much God loves us. Satan is loved no more. That is his truth, not yours!

God loved the world so much that He gave His only Son so that you would be with Him forever.

[1] "That evening they brought to him many who were oppressed by demons, and He cast out the spirits with a word and healed all who were sick." (Matthew 8:16, ESV)

[2] "Your words are so powerful that they will kill or give life…." (Proverbs 18:21, TPT)

[3] "And the angels who did not stay within their own position of authority, but left their proper dwelling, He has been kept in eternal chains under gloomy darkness until the judgment of the great day." (Jude 1:6, ESV)

[4] "you were filled with violence, and you sinned. So I drove you in disgrace from the mount of God, and I expelled you, guardian cherub, from among the fiery stones. Your heart became proud on account of your beauty, and you corrupted your wisdom because of your splendor. So I threw you to the earth." (Ezekiel 28:16–17, NIV)

Chapter 11

Encountering the Spiritual Realm

Chapter Outline:

- What is the Spiritual Realm?
- Psalm 82: The Gods Have Fallen
- Change the Way You Think

What is the Spiritual Realm?

Sometimes I get lost in the spirit realm (in a good way). I watch colossal flying angels with energy swords swoop down to crush the demonic forces. Sometimes I fly on the back of an enormous white dragon! Sometimes I watch an army of trained creatures rushing through the enemy's camp.

The spirit realm is incredible and beyond our understanding! Jesus crushes my box—my opinions—by letting me know that there is so much more than what we see, and He rules it all! As I watched an army of angels blow up a demonic camp without any struggle, the Lord told me, "Micah, you were created for even greater things than they were! Your greatest enemy is doubt. Your box keeps you from reaching above every realm into the greatness that I have made for you."

The spirit realm is real; there is so much happening that sometimes I stay awake all night caught up in God's world. I say this to remind you to crush your boxes, get rid of your opinions, and reach for your full potential in God!

Holy Spirit said, "Son, I need a church that has lost its mind, and instead has the mind of Christ.[1] Get out of your mind and into the Kingdom of God." It is not that studying Scripture or holding to sound theology is wrong, but the desire for everything to fit into my intellectual framework of who God "should" be and how He "should" work limits my perception of Him.

The spirit realm is not a make-believe world. Just as John 14:2 says that there are many mansions in God's house and Revelation 4 describes God sitting on the structure of a throne, there are also buildings, cities, laws, government, and other structures in the spirit realm (Ephesians 6:12).

Although the spirit realm is invisible to natural eyes, you can see the effects naturally. For example, a city in the natural world with a distinctive characteristic may reveal the activity that is happening there in the spirit realm.

The spirit world or spirit realm was created BEFORE this physical realm of Earth.[2] You existed in God before the Earth was made.[3]

You may not realize that people are meant to be the focus of the spirit realm and the physical realm. Adam's original mandate: to be fruitful and multiply and rule.[4] God intended this ruling or authority to be in kingdoms and realms.

Because you have been given this authority by God, what you do and say literally affects things around you in ALL the realms. We need to understand our identity! We need to start thinking bigger about ourselves, otherwise, we are limiting our God-intended influence.

There are not just angels and demons in the spirit realm, there are also other spiritual beings. The spiritual beings who live in the spirit realm know a lot about us. Because we were created to influence them, spiritual beings want to understand humans.

In order to understand how the spirit realm works you need to be aware of the three heavens described in the Bible. Notice in Genesis 1:1 that God created the heavens and the earth. Heavens, not one Heaven. The first heaven is what we might call "sky", an expanse that separates the waters above from the waters below as described in Genesis 1:6–10.[5] The second heaven is where angels and demons war as described in Ephesians 6:12, where prophetic people get their revelation, and where psychics illegally get their information from demonic sources.[6]

God's throne is in the third Heaven, which is a literal place, as shown in Revelation 4:

> "After these things I looked, and behold, a door standing open in heaven. And the first voice which I heard was like a trumpet speaking with me, saying, "Come up here, and I will show you things which must take place after this." Immediately I was in the Spirit, and behold, a throne set in heaven, and One sat on the throne." (Revelation 4:1–2, NKJV)

In the spirit realm there are principalities. They don't like each other. The principalities rule over territories or kingdoms in the spirit realm. These kingdoms are in chaos.

When they fight, riots will break out in cities on the earth. The spirit realm affects the natural realm!

Psalm 82: The Gods Have Fallen

Based on the passage of Psalm 82, The Lord took me to the council of the holy ones, the Elohim, who had once served God. It was the task of these spiritual beings to govern the nations, but they had failed. The Lord allowed me to see these events supernaturally. The magnitude of such experiences is far too great to put clearly into words, but I will do the best I can.

Please read Psalm 82 before you read the encounter:

> "God stands in the congregation of the mighty;
> He judges among the gods.
> How long will you judge unjustly,
> And show partiality to the wicked? Selah
> Defend the poor and fatherless;
> Do justice to the afflicted and needy.
> Deliver the poor and needy;
> Free them from the hand of the wicked.
>
> They do not know, nor do they understand;
> They walk about in darkness;
> All the foundations of the earth are unstable.
>
> I said, "You are gods,
> And all of you are children of the Most High.
> But you shall die like men,
> And fall like one of the princes."
>
> Arise, O God, judge the earth;

For You shall inherit all nations." (Psalm 82, NKJV)

I heard a loud voice shout, "Come!" Yahweh stood in the highest seat in a temple far too magnificent to describe. His presence filled the entire room, which seemed to have no walls or ceiling. His throne was the highest of all thrones and none of the great ones He created could sit in His seat.

Father's appearance was grander than a star of glory. Eternity flowed from the center of His chest like a river to the realms and heavens below. Under His feet was crystal stone, sparkling like the most radiant jewel I have ever seen. His hair was white like a lightning storm in full strength. His garment was a whirlwind of dazzling light and fire! As extraordinary as His face was, I do not have words to describe it other than to say that it was shapes and colors I do not understand. He was beyond beautiful! I fell to the ground on my face before Him.

Again, He said, "Come!" He called with a voice like thunder, and before my eyes, I saw thrones appear, set in place around Yahweh, the uncreated God. Lightning struck these thrones and the Elohim appeared.

Then in a flash, each of the Elohim changed into a figure of white light. I could not see any features accurately, but I could tell they appeared more human than before. Some carried the glory of the Lord, but some who had been disobedient carried darkness. This darkness was growing as they increased their longing for worship.

Yahweh commanded, "Be seated!" Then He opened His mouth, and I could see the entire universe, dimensions, and many spiritual realms as He spoke to the council. In the center, before the throne, was a giant tree with vibrant green leaves! A halo of light shone all around it. I knew this was the Tree of Life as I could feel the presence of the Lord strongly from it. Suddenly, Jesus stepped from within the tree in glory.

Jesus, however, looked different this time though I could still recognize Him. In glory, He gestured to His Father with a slight head bow and then continued.

Jesus said, "I have summoned you because some of you have not been obedient to what We have asked. Your command was not only to rule your dimensions of the spirit world but also to govern the nations in righteousness."

Yahweh continued, "You have failed. Some of you have sought worship. Did I not scatter the people and command you to govern them? Now you have abused your authority and power in order to receive worship." Yahweh's eyes burned with fire. "You have failed."

Jesus spoke, "How would you like to answer for your crimes against worship?"

The Elohim were silent. Those who had disobeyed lowered their heads. The ones who remained faithful continued to look into the eyes of their Creator.

Father asked, "How long am I to deal with you? How long will you stir the nations toward wickedness?" Father's eyes turned toward one of the gods, "You who stir the nations toward sexual pleasure, who manipulate the men in evil passions, did I not dress you in robes of light and crown you with justice? Now you confuse the people and walk unjustly. My fire shall consume you!"

Father turned to another, "You who call yourself 'the storm god', the one who brings the rains, what power do you have? I am the one who opens and closes the heavens."

Yahweh convicted those who had betrayed their original purpose one by one. Yahweh stood from His seat, "Did I not make you all gods, sons of the Most High? All of you were created to stand before me and do justice in my name. You were designed to give wisdom to the nations and guide them through the darkness in my name. But now you have grieved me. You have become a burden to this council in the spirit realm."

Jesus' body burned with a raging fire far too powerful for me to describe. His voice thundered, "Now you will die like men. You have become like dust."

The throne became a firestorm! I fell to the ground to hide from what was about to happen. The faithful and the fallen Elohim took cover from the firestorm that crashed upon them. I covered my head and wept from hearing the gods crying out toward their Creator. It was a noise I will never forget.

A voice came from the throne, "Arise O God, judge the earth; You shall inherit the nations for You created them."

Within the storm, I saw Yahweh hold a sword of light. It was far more powerful than any sword I have ever seen. It dripped with hot molten lava in golden light. Sparks of lightning struck the crystal floor. I looked to find Jesus in the storm but did not see Him. A voice came to me again, "Micah, Jesus is the sword." Father raised the sword and prepared to use it.

I cried out! "Oh, no! I am going to die with them. Help me! Someone, please help me! Father, have mercy on me." I looked back into those eyes of fire. For a moment, Father looked back at me.

Father declared to the Elohim, "Today, I cast you out of my presence. All of you shall die!" Father struck the crystal pavement, and everything exploded. I saw the very foundation of the spiritual realm shift and even the realms of glory become dim as Yahweh's judgment tore open a dimension into darkness. I heard the gods mourn loudly as something was leaving them. I cannot describe it. Something was leaving them. My words fail me, but I saw the true glory of God stripped from them.

As Yahweh tore open the black hole with His power, I was able to catch a glimpse of one of the faithful beings in his human form. Even though terror gripped him, his hands touched my head as if to say, "It is not over. You will help us again. Show us how real sons worship Yahweh."

I was covered by wings. All the fire and glass went around me. Father's eyes were still on me. Then He turned His attention to the gods, and with a voice like thunder He shouted, "Get out!" Yahweh scattered the gods like shooting stars! Away they went from His presence. Yahweh crushed their seats with a terrible lightning strike and a dust cloud covered the room. The ground split open, and the waters fell toward the earth.

I remained protected. The fire of God calmed, and suddenly Satan appeared in his princely attire. He walked forward, shaking his head. His shaded golden wings dragged the floor. He could not hide his real appearance before the Lord.

Satan mocked God, "Once more you have failed, oh King of Kings. What makes you think your children will ever love you?" He laughed. "You are a failure—so emotional. You always get upset when you don't have your way, oh King of Kings, God of all gods!" He bowed while twiddling his fingers.

Satan said, "Your children will never worship you. I will make sure of it. I will now go and manipulate the gods and they will work for me—those who are foolish enough to do so. I will be exalted above you, and you will bow to me." Satan turned into a hellish prince, so dark, twisted, and alone. His cold dark eyes bled with such pride that I could hardly look at him.

Father leaned down to face Satan and with great power He said, "Get out, Satan. Now!" His eyes burned again. "Your time has not yet come."

Satan quickly disappeared.

Father's gaze turned toward me as He held the sword of the Lord, "Micah, go and rest. Remember what you have seen. Tell my priests that the battle for worship is coming to an end. I will be exalted among the nations. The fallen gods have lost all authority and pure worship to me will remove them forever."

I asked, "Lord, what about those who were faithful to You? Some of the gods still loved You."

Father answered, "They will find another purpose, even if they must wander the earth. I know they will find it.

They shall be restored. They will spread the worship of Yahweh to every nation. My Son has made the way!"

Change the Way You Think

For a month the Lord has been visiting me in the night from around 12 a.m. to 4 a.m. with angelic visitations and open heavens. I was asked to record these encounters as they were to help equip the body of Christ! Please know that these are straight out of my journal as the Lord wanted me to share them this way.

A Prophet with Identity Issues

In the middle of the night, I saw a vision of a Prophet opening his mouth to vomit bones and decaying flesh. Jesus stood next to me and said, "This is what a Prophet looks like when he has identity issues. Stop begging to be heard; you get in the way when you do this. People are meant to listen to my voice, not yours. Keep yourself in me and you won't look like this. If you live in a spirit of rejection, you end up getting in my way. It's not about you; it is about me!"

Jesus' eyes were on fire as He said this phrase to me, "Prophets who live in rejection can easily become tools for the enemy...."

I am Not Your Butler

This encounter may be a challenging word for some, but I need to share it.

In the middle of the night, a solemn angel appeared in my room dressed in noble attire. He had a staff in his hand which emitted the glory of God. He said, "I am not your butler! The angels are not your butlers. We answer the voice of the Lord and obey His will. There must be a culture of honor when it comes to the angelic ministry!"

He was very serious about this, and his voice shook my room. We must properly honor and respect the angelic ministry if we wish to work with them appropriately.

Not Your Choice to Send the Angels

In the middle of the night, I saw an archangel standing over my bed! He said to me, "Listen to what I have to say. For more time than your given years to breathe, I have been trained to protect you and lead the group of angels assigned to you! It is not your choice to send the angels but God's!" He looked down at me while holding his blazing helmet in his right arm, "We train and learn just as you do. We are prepared to work with you, as you are prepared to work with us! Your Father releases us when He decides."

Father, thank you for the angels you have assigned to us! Thank you for preparing your body to work alongside the angels like never before!

Restoration

I am pondering the spirit realm. it's so real... so full of life and very sad. It is a realm of light, beauty, and life, but also darkness, sadness, and brokenness. Sometimes when I walk about observing the spirit realm around me, I can see that it too is going to be restored one day. I am so thankful that Jesus is going to fix things forever! Even the spirit realm won't remain the same!

Jesus, thank you so much for restoring all things! I love you!

Breaking Our Boxes

Jesus showed me a beautiful box! I mean this box was terrific in detail: a gorgeous ribbon adorned it, and I couldn't wait to see what was inside. Jesus held this box before me, saying, "Micah, isn't this a nice box? It has excellent detail, nice colors... it appears to have everything."

Before I could comment on the box, Jesus crushed it into dust!

Oh, the pain I felt....

Then His voice was like thunder, "Tell my people I do not like their boxes! I do not like their ways and I will not give in to their blackmail. Micah, it is my kingdom come, my will be done! I am not interested in their kingdoms, their rule... I will crush them! Tell them I will not be contained in their boxes."

I was shaking from the authority with which He spoke! I fell on my face before Him as He said, "My Kingdom is growing and intensifying. Son, those who cannot partner with me will need to move quickly...."

Don't Prophesy to Validate Yourself

In a recent visit to Heaven, the Prophet Isaiah expressed this to me:

"When you prophesy to validate yourself, you become a liar. When you combine your gift with the desire to please man you are stepping into a religious spirit. Holy Spirit is not interested in pleasing you, but in making you more like Jesus. When you prophesy to bring validation to your ministry you are removing its purpose, which is to glorify Jesus. Stop trying to prove who you are or what you are sent to do! When you let Holy Spirit do His work, He will also back you up if needed."

You Don't Need to Be Right

In Heaven one day, Holy Spirit challenged me, "Micah, trying to be right can sometimes keep you from hearing my truth! You don't need to be right; you need to be humbled. I can't work with anyone who would rather be right. I work with the weak, broken, and humble-hearted. Stop trying to be right."

My chest burned… ouch!

Starve the Demons

At around 1 in the morning, I finally laid down to sleep when I suddenly entered the spirit world. Holy Spirit, who appeared next to me, touched my shoulder to get my attention, "Understand what I am about to say to you, Micah. Write it down in your heart and record it in your realm." He took me to the most disgusting pond I had ever seen. It was black and slimy and gave off an awful aroma. I didn't even want to be close to the borders of this terrible pond, yet Holy Spirit insisted that I look. I got on my hands and knees to look into the waters, where I saw demons swimming. They had protruding eyes and terrible teeth. They resembled piranhas, but with legs instead of fins. They watched me as they were looking for food.

Holy Spirit said, "They feed on sin, Micah. When you live in sin, refraining from a heart of repentance, demons feed off you to sustain their life. They drain your joy, peace, and many other wonderful things that I have given you. Demons will have authority in your life if you do not repent and change your way."

The demonic beings hissed as Holy Spirit spoke again, "Starving them is how you get rid of them, but you must also get rid of the pond of filth. You must change your lifestyle. Telling them to go is not enough when you are not walking in repentance. Resisting the devil is walking in truth, which is living in repentance. Turn and change your way to my truth or demons will feast until there is nothing left at all!"

Holy Spirit touched my shoulder and smiled, "Now, go back and tell them what you have seen and heard!"

[1] "For who has understood the mind of the Lord so as to instruct Him?" But we have the mind of Christ." (1 Corinthians 2:16, ESV)

² "Before I formed you in the womb, I knew you" (Jeremiah 1:5, ESV)

³ "For you formed my inward parts; you knitted me together in my mother's womb." (Psalm 139:13, ESV)

⁴ "And God blessed them. And God said to them, "Be fruitful and multiply and fill the earth and subdue it and have dominion over the fish of the sea and over the birds of the heavens and over every living thing that moves on the earth." (Genesis 1:28, ESV)

⁵ "...And God said, "Let there be an expanse in the midst of the waters, and let it separate the waters from the waters." And God made the expanse and separated the waters that were under the expanse from the waters that were above the expanse. And it was so. And God called the expanse Heaven...." (From Genesis 1:6–10, ESV)

⁶ "For we do not wrestle against flesh and blood, but against the rulers, against the authorities, against the cosmic powers over this present darkness, against the spiritual forces of evil in the heavenly places." (Ephesians 6:12, ESV)

Chapter 12

Declaring from the Heart of God

Chapter Outline:

- The Voice of the Lord
- The Kiss: Jesus
- The Kiss: The Father
- The Kiss: Holy Spirit

The Voice of the Lord

I went to a prayer meeting and noticed that there were strong angels standing against the walls—very buff, built angels with weapons. Some had large spears with lightning coming out of them and fire all over them and those were just the weapons that made sense to me. They also had weapons that I don't know how to describe. Some had very strong wings of metal, and some didn't have wings… but they were large and lined up against the wall and they looked like they were waiting. I wanted to figure out what was going on because the angels weren't moving in response to that prayer meeting. The people were declaring and prophesying things that sounded great, but the angels weren't moving. I didn't want to look creepy, so I walked to the wall and whispered to one of them, trying to talk with my mouth closed, and asked, "What are you guys doing?"

The angel, who had his arms crossed, looked down at me with very serious eyes. I remember he had very thick black eyebrows and brown eyes, and said, "We only listen to the voice of the Lord, and we don't hear it." That disturbed me because everyone thought they were hearing the Lord and prophesying but they were not. In the Bible, it says, "Bless the Lord, you His angels, mighty in strength, who perform His word, obeying the voice of His word!" (Psalm 103:20, NASB 1995)

Eventually, a little girl came up and said one simple prayer. As she finished, the angels shot forward in blinding light and carried her prayer quickly! They were launched with one simple prayer!

I learned that the way we operate with angels and how accurately we operate with them depends on us listening to God's voice, really knowing God, and being intimate with Him. Then the angels will recognize His voice in us and will launch and do what they are assigned to do. The key is knowing the Lord's voice, knowing Him intimately. You can't just command angels because they don't listen to you, they listen to God and obey Him. God will give angels the assignment, "What I say through this person, you will do," and release them on that assignment, but it's our connection with God that launches them.

The Kiss: Lord Jesus

I was feeling lost and abandoned one day, and at the end of my strength. I cried out to God for help. It had been some time since I had seen the Lord Jesus and I missed Him. Nothing will ever take His place. As I cried out to God for strength because the warfare was too thick, His voice broke in, "Micah, I am with you!" His voice opened the realm of Heaven, and I was launched into the brightness of His glory—beyond the stars and all dimensions—into His presence of warm light. But I still did not see Him.

I was standing by a river of life. It was a beautiful crystal light with rainbow fish swimming about. I had been there before; I recognized the land. The leaves, gorgeous in red and gold, fell on me and into the river flowing from the throne of God. All rivers flow from the throne of God because He is the river of life. It comes from within His presence and deep inside the throne.[1] Even though I didn't see Him yet, I waited upon the Lord. I knew He would come because this was always our place of meeting. I stepped into the water to relax when I heard Him walking behind me.

My sweet Lord Jesus… I could smell Him as He approached me from behind. I did not look… I just closed my eyes and waited for His embrace! I rested in the fragrance coming from Him: frankincense, vanilla, and roses. His fragrance opened me up to His love! He embraced me. His cheek touched mine and then He kissed my ear with His words, saying, "I am always right here, Micah." He turned me around so that I could look into His eyes of love, and He said, "Tell me, who has my Father's eyes?"

I shouted, "I do!" I was thrilled, "I have my Father's eyes!" He kissed them and brought me closer for another embrace. I don't remember how long I stayed there with Him… it is beyond description. Jesus is amazing! He is so full of beauty and light! His robe is like a sea of crystal sparkling in the sunlight. His hair is white with glory from the Father's love and joy upon Him! I felt His groomed beard touch my face and then sadness came from His heart for a moment.

"Jesus," I looked to see His eyes, "What is it?"

After a deep sigh, He pulled me closer to hear His words, "I never want you to feel abandoned, Micah. It is not true. I remember the day I made you. I remember the day you moved in the palm of my Father's hand. On that day I showed you who your parents would be because I was filled with joy and longed to send you as a gift to them. I watched you and loved you from the beginning of time, son. The enemy's greatest feeling is loneliness because he was indeed cast out. But you, my child, are never cast out! I have joined my heart to yours—I have walked inside you and you inside me."

His words touched me so deeply! I looked around Him to see that the red and golden trees had circled us. They created a beautiful canopy around the Lord and me. When I looked back at Jesus His face was so bright that I could no longer see His features. He pulled my face toward Him until our noses touched. He said with a gentle kiss, "Micah, I love you! Tell my people I love them. I love them, and they are not forgotten or cast out. I am always with them. They place their love in so many things just so they can feel a connection, but they were made to connect to God. Only I can bring real healing! I will come and heal them, my child, as I am healing you.[2] I know the battles are hard and I know death tries to steal what it should not have. But I have conquered death so that I may spend eternity with them. I want my bride—I want my bride to rest right on my heart. Intimacy with me… the eternal love."

He chuckled as our heads touched, "Nothing will ever take your place, son. I am drawn by the beauty from within your spirit. By light I come, and with joy, I sing. My dance is the symphony of love from your heart."

I asked Him, "Jesus, you like the song I bring?" I placed my hands on His chest to feel His heartbeat. "I don't know what it sounds like. I can't hear it."

He smiled with His shining blue eyes. He sighed again with relief! I guess He wanted me to know this. "Come with me, son, into my Father's throne so that He may kiss you now," He said, pulling me upstream with excitement.

I laughed because I was surprised that Father God wanted to give me a kiss too. Jesus turned to me, "I believe the first one who held you should have the chance to kiss you, don't you think?" He winked at me and continued to lead me upstream toward the throne that appeared out of the deep golden light. I could see the face of God with His eyes of blue fire watching me draw near.

"You are fairer than the sons of men; Grace is poured upon Your lips; Therefore God has blessed You forever." (Psalm 45:2, NASB 1995)

"My beloved is dazzling and ruddy, Outstanding among ten thousand." (Song of Solomon 5:10, NASB 1995)

"And He was transfigured before them. His face shone like the sun, and His clothes became as white as the light." (Matthew 17:2, NASB 1995)

The Kiss: God the Father

Jesus led me toward the Father's throne of light where I saw
His glory reflected off His glass-like robe. Beautiful depictions
of His glory are beyond my description, but each wave of light
spoke to me. Voices that came from the throne of light joined
my spirit with fire! Jesus held my hand as He guided me
upstream and deep into the light. "Come, Micah, the kiss of
God awaits you." We climbed up golden steps with water
flowing down into the river below. It was an enchanting
invitation to draw near Him; He is the fountain of life![3] Jesus
and I entered the throne when suddenly everything became
pure white, and Jesus disappeared.

When the white smoke had lifted, a great angel with
large pearl wings stepped forward holding a book in his hand.
His robe was the color of roses, and his head was composed of
gems shining like a rainbow. He announced, "Welcome, son
of light!" He seemed to have an occupation before the throne
of God, but I did not ask. He walked right through me and
faded away. I stepped forward on my own deeper into the
throne; how strange yet beautiful. Water, clear as crystal, was
the surface of the throne room but it was only ankle deep and
mist hovered above it. Everything was so bright and glorious
with great clouds composed of light floating above me as if
they were hiding someone. As I walked forward, the clouds
closed behind me and then opened in front of me to display
the glory of God. My breath was taken while bliss
overwhelmed me. I cannot put into words how great God is—
His glory is undeniably beautiful. His large fiery-blue eyes
pierced my soul with love that only God can give. His face
was like diamonds—much like the robe of Jesus—with
hundreds of rays of light coming out of Him. He was looking

right at me with an intensity of joy. His robe was like the clouds hovering around Him with lightning flashing. My Father smiled at me and blew on my face.

"Receive, my son," His voice was thunderous but gentle. It can be heard throughout Heaven, but it is not unpleasant—it is the most powerful and humbling voice you can experience. His voice is so close to you that it sounds like He is right next to your ear. He doesn't hurt your ears, but His voice is in your ear. "Receive my love and come closer."

I took a deep breath to absorb His gift to me: His breath of life. I took one step forward and I was picked up by His hand and brought to His chest. I looked at His glorious face and did not turn away. With His right hand, He poured oil on me that smelled like honey. I noticed that the oil was coming from His head, which is the joy of the Lord. I just rested while Father ministered to me the way He wanted to. Father's great diamond-like hands brushed my hair back—He was bathing me in His oil. He said to me, "This is the oil I poured out over my Son before He left my presence to enter the Earth. It was to prepare Him for His burial. That is why it was so meaningful when the woman poured out her fragrance upon Jesus. It reminded my Son of me." He continued to wash me in His oil while looking into my eyes. I cannot explain the feeling of looking into the eyes of God the Father. He sees everything— believes in everything, you are as His son. The Trinity made you with all their love and joy. I reached for His face, and He closed His eyes to receive from me. I blew kisses toward Father's face till His undoing. With His eyes closed peacefully, He spoke, "I receive it, Micah."

I rested my head back while Father held me with His hands, still allowing the sweet oil to run over my body. He said, "On the day of your beginning, I washed you in my love. I spoke purpose into you... I prepared your life to be an image of my Son, Jesus. You have been crucified with Christ, the flesh laid into a tomb, and have been risen with Christ. I know you, Micah!"⁴ He leaned in to kiss my lips again and again and again.

Father said, "My light is your garment, Micah. The cloud of gentleness is the manifest breath of God. Tell my children to beware of deception. The enemy comes to preach another god. One that says, 'You can have all your will, and God will be satisfied.' No! I desire that my will and pleasure be in you, son. There is a great rebellion coming from those who listen to the enemy's voice. Their hair, or wisdom, has become sullied by the lies the enemy has spoken to them. They have devoured the ways of the flesh."

When He said this, I suddenly saw visions of demons teaching some of His children how to live in the flesh and still be ok with God. These demons were dressed in white, but they had teeth like bats and no eyes. Their skin was rotting away. Then I saw the wisdom of some become ruined. Father said as the vision left me, "Those are my teachers who have the gift to understand my will but who listened to the enemy's voice instead. They must repent because I will hold them accountable for teaching lies. Clean up, my teachers... my fire is coming!" He smiled, "I am a forgiving God, my son."

He was silent for a moment watching my every move, like a Father holding a baby in His arms. Tears of joy fell on me—even on my lips. They were sweet. I could smell them too; fragrant oils of Heaven are His tears.

Father wiped my tears with His left hand and shouted, "Come!" And He pulled me into a realm of dreams. He held my hand as we walked through fields of orbs that floated past us. He said with joy, "These small lights are my dreams. I call this place 'The Field of Dreams' and this is the reason you see my thoughts. I created you to connect with me more deeply than you know. Through your dreams, you encounter mine— hidden realities and truths about me that I give to you. I have desires, my son. I do not even tell the angels until I tell my children first. Some things they will not know until I release them to my children." He tightened His squeeze as He held my hand, "I am so glad to show you this, Micah. Dreams are going to increase this year to those who consecrate their eyes to me." This place was beautiful: a field of floating orbs everywhere! Golden trees with leaves dipped in blue surrounded us while pillars of light reached high into the twilight sky. The grass was painted like a rainbow, and millions of orbs contained little whispers from Father's heart.

I saw Holy Spirit swirling around this place calling my name. He brought an orb just for me. I reached for it—it was about the size of a basketball! It was so alive and breathing! Father said, "This is one of the many dreams I have for you, Micah." He laughed, "I can't wait for you to see what it is!" He placed me on His shoulder, and we continued our walk through the Fields of Dreams.

The Kiss: Holy Spirit

A great wind had blown past me as I sat on Father's shoulder; He grinned with such pleasure—all He wanted to do was be with me! I could hear the voices of mysteries within the orbs of light in the Field of Dreams! Each one contained the very beginning of eternity as if it had its own grasp on the fabric of reality within the dimensions of life! Father looked at me and said, "Each dream I give is a gift for you to see into eternity; holiness is eternity. Holiness is in the DNA of your spirit."

As we continued our walk Holy Spirit spoke, "By my sweet voice, I nursed you. I nursed you in the womb of God, and I was with you in the womb of your mother. I harvested the dreams of the Father and placed each one inside you so that you would fulfill all of them."[5]

The sweet voice of Holy Spirit was very soothing to my soul, and I remembered His nearness to me from my beginning; how strange… but beautiful. I was never alone!

The wind continued to circle us, and I could see the beautiful colors of Heaven that sparkled in the brilliant twilight sky. The wind was reachable. This wind is what gave my body the ability to be… it is the breath that entered my being, the rhythm of my heartbeat. The wind lifted us up to the very cosmos of Heaven with millions of stars. There were angels surrounded by countless dreams, hovering by the eternal wisdom of God!

Holy Spirit said, "My kiss to you, son of light, is that you would understand the mystery of His love and that you would be bathed in the unquenchable fire of His passion for you! I saw the gathering of stars come from great and beautiful wings full of eyes and this is what Holy Spirit said, "I have given a gift to mankind to see and to understand the mind of God, to see deep into dreams and draw unshakable revelation to the listening ear.[6] Are you ready for me to come and kiss your ear? Are you ready for me to come and kiss the eyes of your heart? My kisses are fire; my kiss is like the unpredictable wind!"

The great wings I saw in this dimension in the Field of Dreams began to utter the word "holy" over and over! Then millions of angels began to respond to those who had said "Yes!" A great flash of light appeared to the right of Father introducing Jesus to the scene. He smiled at me with blue eyes of love and said, "It was in our dreams that you would be one with the Trinity and nothing else. Out of our being comes unity! That you would be in me and I in you, thus causing the body to be one! You are one in us first, Micah, because this is where you began." When Jesus spoke, all the knowledge and dreams of God rested upon Him and He said, "To some, I have given Apostles, some Prophets, Teachers, Shepherds, and Evangelists so that you may grow up in the knowledge of God, my son."[7]

Holy Spirit's voice came from the wind again, "I am the breath that sustains you to encounter... to behold."

Father, who held me on His shoulder, laughed with great joy as it rolled through the cosmos. The angels smiled as well, and the stars flickered with the giggles of little children. He said, "I want to let you fly, Micah! It is time to fly." He took me off His shoulder, released me into the cosmos of Heaven, and His voice thundered, "Go and kiss the world with the love of God, Micah!"

The wind lifted me deep into the revelation of my Father—the home of mankind—His heart. His dreams. His kiss! Deep calls unto deep... where shall man hide? Where shall man lay His head? Into the dreams of God.

When I returned to earth, I sat up to look out my window at the portal in the sky! I could see angels dashing by the portal, creating ribbons of light in the air. Holy Spirit said, "They go to those who sleep! His children carry the dreams given to them by God. Get ready for revelations so profound that it takes the God of Light to reveal the mysteries! Yes, the angels have come." I felt a hand of fire on my left shoulder. It was Holy Spirit standing right next to me looking out the window. His face was made of golden light. I could not see His features but knew that He was happy! He looked at this scene with me until I saw Him no more!

How plentiful are the dreams of God–like the starry skies of night. Endless wonder exists in the Field of Dreams.

[1] "Then the angel showed me the river of the water of life, bright as crystal, flowing from the throne of God and of the Lamb." (Revelation 22:1, ESV)

[2] "He himself bore our sins in His body on the tree, that we might die to sin and live to righteousness. By His wounds you have been healed." (1 Peter 2:24, ESV)

[3] "and you give them drink from the river of your delights for with you is the fountain of life; in your light do we see light." (Psalm 36:8–9, ESV)

[4] "O Lord, you have searched me and known me! You know when I sit down and when I rise up; you discern my thoughts from afar. You search out my path and my lying down and are acquainted with all my ways." (Psalm 139:1–3, ESV)

[5] "Even before we were born, God planned in advance our destiny and the good works we would do to fulfill it!" (Ephesians 2:10, TPT)

[6] "Be transformed by the renewal of your mind, that by testing you may discern what is the will of God, what is good and acceptable and perfect." (Romans 12:2, ESV)

[7] "And He gave the apostles, the prophets, the evangelists, the shepherds and teachers, to equip the saints for the work of ministry, for building up the body of Christ, until we all attain to the unity of the faith and of the knowledge of the Son of God" (Ephesians 4:11–13, ESV)

Read More!

Enjoy more of Micah Turnbo's encounters at **beholdwonder.com** *The Behold Wonder website contains blog posts, devotionals, podcasts, and videos.*

Author Bio

Micah is a Seer Prophet, founder of Behold Wonder and the Pastor of Prophetic Ministry at Vineyard Church Northwest in Cincinnati, Ohio. He grew up in a very prophetic family where spending time with God was a normal part of homeschooling, and then continued his education at Cincinnati Christian University and International House of Prayer in Kansas City, Missouri (IHOPKC).

Micah's mission is to encourage people to connect to the heart of God and his goal is to see friends of God encounter Him in a real way so that His display of glory and power is recognized across the earth.

Acknowledgements

Many thanks to Kendra Barrow for the content editing, Mary Tews and Hazel Lebrun for being the editing team, Keith Froelich for the cover art, and Cameron Suter for strategic help with the book cover.

URGENT PLEA!

Thank you for reading my book!

I really appreciate all your feedback and
I love hearing what you have to say.

I need your input to make the next version of this
book and my future books even better.

Please take two minutes now to leave a helpful review on
Amazon to let me know what you think of the book.

Thanks so much!
— Micah Turnbo

Made in the USA
Monee, IL
07 May 2023

33106098R00121